THEMES OF CATECHESIS

Themes of Catechesis

Marcel van Caster, S.J.

BURNS & OATES/HERDER AND HERDER

BURNS & OATES LIMITED
25 Ashley Place, London, S.W.1

First published in Great Britain 1967

Original edition: *Dieu Nous Parle, 2. Thèmes de la Catéchèse,*
Bruges, Desclée De Brouwer, 1965.
This translation was made by Olga Guedatarian.

Disc No. : 78292

© 1967 by Herder and Herder, Inc.

Reproduced and printed in Great Britain by
Billing and Sons Limited, Guildford and London

Contents

CONTENTS

Introduction

THE word of God, which catechesis must make known to men, is a coherent whole. Too often, the subject matter of a religion course is presented as being something distinct from the Christian message. However, the subject matter of a religion course, which we here present as the "main themes" of catechesis, traverses the entire message, and indeed, in a catechetical sense at least, is the message. Catechesis, therefore, must speak continuously of God, of Jesus Christ, of his Church, the Eucharist, faith, charity, eschatology.

The present work is closely related to another book, *The Structure of Catechetics*.* It is our hope, in fact, that the reader of this book will have already read the first, for it is there that we have elaborated the general framework in which the themes of the Christian message are to be presented.

For the purpose of helping the catechist to integrate and synthesize his catechesis the more easily, we have thought it best to adopt the same plan of inquiry for each theme. This method

* New York, Herder and Herder, 1965.

was also chosen because the sources for our catechesis on each theme are largely the same sources—though, of course, in varying degrees. Thus, under the chapter section entitled "God's Word," we discuss, in turn, how God's word on a theme is to be found in the Bible, in the liturgy, in Christian witness, and finally in doctrinal reflection. A second section attempts to show how man, in his psychological and sociological conditioning, is prepared, or not prepared, to receive God's word. Lastly, a third part hopes to provide the catechist with insights on how he can best prepare and proceed with his catechesis on the particular theme under discussion.

A disadvantage in such a divisioning of chapters is that it might appear to be too systematic an approach—and, as we are all aware, the practice of system is the death of catechesis. Or it may appear that we are trying to delimit to certain specific areas of research all that can be said in an important way about a particular theme. We take these risks, however, hopeful that before long the reader will come to realize that we are offering here a creative, existential catechesis—for it is God's *living* word which must be proclaimed; and that we chose to confine ourselves to certain major areas of discussion only because it is over-all the more convenient and helpful.

THEMES OF CATECHESIS

I

God

1. GOD'S WORD

THE living God is revealed both in his actions and through them, as well as through the task he has entrusted to his "spokesmen" of proclaiming and interpreting (which is to say, of declaring) the divine intervention in history. Moreover, he makes it possible for man to encounter him in a special way in the symbols he has instituted. These we confront in three ways: through the experience of events, which we will here call "life witness"; through the celebration of the liturgy; and through the formulation of doctrine. Our vocabulary of "experience," "celebration," and "formulation" is not an arbitrary one, for in fact the trilogy history-liturgy-doctrine forms the very groundwork of catechesis. All of our themes are focused here. We can say, therefore, that man comes to know the word of God mainly by means of life witness, worship, doctrinal formulation, and, in conjunction with all three, the revelation of God's word in the Bible.

The Bible

The three basic forms of God's word are to be found in the Bible, and the chief of these is the existential. The other two forms, symbolic and statementive, will not be elaborated on here since we will have occasion to discuss them more fully later on.

The Bible is a continuous catechesis based on events and their significance. By "events" we mean historical facts which in some way change the existing situation. There are two kinds of events, namely, religious events, in which God's intervention is more in evidence; and worldly events, that is, events which are not explicitly religious but which have a religious significance through their relationship with religious events. The Bible is arranged as a selection of the principal religious events, some of which took place in a relatively short space of time, others which were spread out over longer periods. Beginning with these events, it is God-in-relation-to-man who reveals himself. Our knowledge of God-in-relation-to-man leads us to a knowledge of God-in-himself. In the New Testament, God reveals that his life-in-himself is one of relationship between three divine Persons. However, if we wish to take the biblical approach to a knowledge of God, we must first of all fix our attention on the *progressive revelation* of the relationship which God enters into with man. He reveals himself in the progressive realization of the "economy" of salvation; this economy, furthermore, is based on "God's ways of acting" towards man. God is constant and faithful in his ways of acting, and this is how we see him in the Bible.

Now these three aspects of divine revelation—God-in-relation-to-man, God-in-himself, and progressive—revelation reach their highest point in the life of Jesus Christ, the perfect mediator.

Biblical catechesis, that is, one which is developed according to the spirit and the categories of the Bible, will, therefore, be at the basis of the events and "themes of relationship" between God and man. But then, a twofold approach in biblical catechesis is possible: we can reflect on an event and read into it the different themes concerning God's way of acting; and we can pursue a theme through the general line of development of biblical events.

An example will help to clarify our meaning. Were the catechist to present the two complementary themes of holiness and benevolence according to the biblical approach, he could begin with the first event recorded in the Bible, creation. Here is a personal God acting and speaking to man. He is both Lord and benefactor. As Lord he has established order, and as benefactor he has made a promise—though on the negative side, he has made a threat as well.

Abraham is the personal summation of God's order and promise. The story of Abraham also introduces the notion of "country"—geological, economic, and religious. The country is order and promise.

In Moses we find God being actively faithful to his promise; his lordly activity is evident in the power over things and over history that he has given to Moses—but his name remains mysterious. Now also the covenant between God and man is made. It is a covenant of order and promise.

David is the living sign of the beneficent sovereignty of God. His reign also evidences the continuity of the messianic promise.

The procedure for the continuation of this double theme should now be easily recognizable.

Jesus Christ brings the full revelation of God in two ways. First, by the acts he accomplishes (and the words he utters) as the envoy of God, he manifests the divine greatness and goodness in his miracles and in the supreme gift of salvation (divine life). Secondly, by his example, and because he takes an active share in our existence, he shows us how we ought to respect and love "our Father who is in heaven and who takes care of all of us."

Jesus is able to send us the Holy Spirit in behalf of the Father because of the interior light which he possesses. We receive here and now, although in the veiled way of faith, the full revelation of God which will be given to us for the perfect contemplation when all salvation is fulfilled. Our knowledge of God is in a perpetual state of growth.

We should keep in mind in our catechesis that the development of a biblical theme which follows the laws of exegesis resembles the explanation of an "attribute" of God as seen in its doctrinal aspect. There is a difference, however, between the biblical and doctrinal explanations. A doctrine which takes for its basis the philosophical notion of "absolute, infinite Being" immediately comes up against difficulties arising from "relationships": one cannot say of the absolute Being that he has a relationship. In the same way, no intervention which is "historical" and therefore limited can ever completely be joined with the notion of an unlimited Being.

One must also be mindful of a similar difference whenever it seems possible to "prolong" a biblical theme into a liturgical theme. As a matter of fact, the laws of the two types—one is existential, the other symbolic—are not the same. A catechesis which would be both biblical and liturgical, therefore, must be sensitive to the "change of key" involved.

By presenting biblical revelation, catechesis already fulfills its threefold task of teaching, training, and initiation for an encounter with God. In fact, it awakens and strengthens faith, which is a "meeting with God through signs." The basic signs are existential: they consist of the great deeds in the history of salvation, especially those concerning the earthly life of Jesus. Since God speaks to us here and now through our contact with the Bible, faith which is set in motion by biblical catechesis will also take on the form of prayer, which is an encounter based

16

on the sense of God's presence. The same process takes place in a special way in the liturgy.

The Liturgy

Let us remind ourselves of the role of the liturgy in catechesis. God is manifested in the liturgy in two ways.

1. The liturgy offers a choice of biblical texts, arranged according to the laws of worship, which are of a symbolic order. This results, further, in a twofold principle of selection in Christian liturgy. Basically, the arrangement of texts rests on the real unity that exists between the facts of the Old and of the New Testament. But it also effects a *"rapprochement"* between those texts whose unifying factor lies in an association of words or ideas— without, of course, there being any claim made on the part of ecclesiastical authorities to give an exegetical interpretation of what God actually meant in these texts.

2. The symbolic action, accompanied by words which make the meaning clear, is a "mediation" for encounter with God. The rite, which is only complete when man takes part in it, is a meeting with God under efficacious symbol; for although the liturgy may not be the only form of actualization of the Christian mystery, it is one which possesses a special efficaciousness, since our Lord instituted it to this end. Moreover, the whole structure of celebration expresses God's approach towards us in Jesus Christ and our approach towards God, which is a share in the Lord's gesture towards his Father in the strength of the Holy Spirit.

The structure of the liturgical year, in each and all of its several parts, also shows us the essential rhythm of the mystery of God who calls us to himself in Jesus Christ.

Numerous texts (lessons, prefaces) which express the different aspects of the Church's faith in God likewise have a place within the sacramental celebration.

Life Witness

There are special ways of acting and speaking in situations and "events" which have some relationship to God, whether in an explicit way (religious events) or implicitly (worldly or "profane" events).

Catechesis which is based on current events of a religious nature is an extension, then, of existential biblical catechesis. An example of behavior in a religious event is the attitude of the Christian believer toward an unbeliever who shows an interest in faith in God; or on the other hand, the attitude of the Christian believer towards an unbeliever who mocks faith in God.

Worldly or profane events, too, belong in the field of "witness," especially when they make us reflect more critically on the meaning of life and the scale of values—on such things as birth and death, great joy or great sorrow, the choice of career, and the predominant motive in the exercise of that career: money, learning, fame, the service of one's neighbor.

Witness, then, is twofold. It includes, on the one hand, the signs of God which show his intervention in the lives of men since biblical times—and we do not mean miracles only, but also and especially the general workings of providence in ordinary circumstances; and on the other hand, the acts by which believers show their faith in God, and the words which interpret these acts. Even though they themselves may be in error,* the

---

* Along these general lines, speaking of the charism of protest, Karl Rahner has said: "So we must be able to have the courage (for this can be the precise function given by the Spirit to a particular member of the Church), to say *No* in the Church, to make a stand against certain trends and spirits, even before the official hierarchy itself has been alarmed. In fact, such a protest can be God's means of rousing his ministers to act. One must have this courage, even if one must tell oneself, knowing the limits of one's own judgment, that probably the further history of the Church will show that one was not entirely right, that one was only one servant among many of the one Lord of the Church, and not the only one to represent him; in fact, that the Lord was also acting in that other person whom one had

believers can be "mediators" through whom God makes himself known to their neighbors. This is true of saints, of converts, of Christians in the world and in religious life, of priests, but especially of the catechist himself, who is in direct contact with those to whom he speaks of God.

Reflection and Formulation

There are contained within the actual knowledge that faith gives several ways of knowing.

The existential signs of God contain and manifest their "meaning," that is, their concrete reality. At this level, thought is direct and can be progressively deepened. The formulation of direct thought is spontaneous and does not have to be constructed by way of a static process.

The normal exercise of our intelligence, however, calls for reflection on the knowledge that we have acquired directly. Reflective thought can proceed, moreover, on its own level, in different ways. Abstraction, for example, results in a notional and systematic doctrine; meditation leads to wisdom which is flexible and which is expressed above all in valid judgment on a variety of situations. In religious teaching, it is important to make use not only of doctrinal statements, but just as much of statements of a sapiential nature.

As regards the theme of God, reflection by way of abstraction offers certain advantages which correspond to a fixed psychological development, but it is quick to fall into the danger of "reducing" the living God to an "object" (neuter) of human thought and discussion. That kind of rigid "doctrinal" presentation, therefore, which considers God merely from without, and which takes no account of his active, interior presence, must be avoided in religious teaching. Efforts have been made to remedy the abstract

the task of putting in his place, and convincing of his limitations." From *The Dynamic Element in the Church*, New York, Herder and Herder, 1964, p. 77.

character of certain dogmas by developing a moral doctrine corresponding to the basic attitudes of man towards God; but while this is good, it is not enough.

Reflection by way of meditation, on the other hand, has the advantage of always being concrete. It refers to facts and to the real values contained in them, whether it is a question of the one who accomplishes these deeds—God in action—or of the one to whom God speaks through these deeds. However, the presentation of these facts and the axiomatic truths they contain remain incomplete for as long as the presentation fails to penetrate to the ontological basis of values, on which true wisdom depends. Hence meditation which brings out the relationship between our innermost being and God must go beyond an anthropocentric philosophy and launch out into an encounter with God, who is transcendent and immanent.

For example, meditation on divine providence should not consist merely in seeing how God responds to our wishes, but, founded on complete trust in God whose ways are not our ways, it should try to understand how well God's ways serve the only purpose which has any real importance.

2. THE HUMAN BACKGROUND

Psychology

We presuppose on the part of the catechist-reader a general acquaintance with the general principles of psychological evolution, and also with the chief psychological characteristics of the various age groups under discussion here.*

In childhood, our idea of God is grounded mainly on his almightiness, especially as it directly relates to the child himself. The child lives in the present. Thus, when he realizes that God's answer to his request is slow in coming, he finds himself faced

* See Chapter 10 of *The Structure of Catechetics*, "Man's Situation," under the headings "Structures in Psychological Development" (pp. 143–145) and "Catechesis of the Different Age-Groups" (pp. 145–149).

with a mystery: God is something other. But he approaches God in faith and trust.

The pre-adolescent soon gains a knowledge of "secondary causes" and their laws. God, the first cause, is abstract, so that the pre-adolescent begins to consider his duties towards him in an impersonal way.

In puberty, the adolescent undergoes interior disturbance and upheaval. What, he asks, does God really want of me? What can I really expect from him?

The older adolescent begins to form a personal relationship with God; and the sense of mystery is revived. There is an intimate connection between his view of God and his outlook on the world.

As man enters into adulthood, he becomes more and more preoccupied with his work. His ideas of God are now related to his marriage, to education, to his ideas for a better world.

With everyone, however, there is always a danger of stagnation. Deviations from the religious sense often correspond to psychological defects—prayer, for instance, is regarded as "magic"; or a person desires to compensate for deficiencies in human affections by assuming a sentimental religiosity; or he might adhere to a moral system that does not have a sufficiently theological basis. Hence the religious sense is often embedded in hypocrisy, routine and apathy, anxiety. Catechesis must help the catechized from becoming bogged down in these defects by showing how an egocentric attitude must continually be "converted" towards an encounter with God in charity.

Sociology

Religious sociology has given us numerous insights into the sources of group mentality, as well as into certain types of mentality which cultural progress brings with it.*

* See under "Religious Sociology," pp. 149–152, in Chapter 10 of *The Structure of Catechetics*.

Certain writers have described in detail the succession of three "civilizations" in human history: the patriarchal, the middle-class, and the technical (or organizational). Each stage has a corresponding idea of God which is valid in certain of its elements but also in need of purification in others. The God of nature, or the paternalist God, or the God of the rationalists, is more or less dead now; it is the living God who now lives. He is mysterious yet close at hand, and he requires the gift of ourselves.

Other writers have demonstrated the consequences of a three-fold revolution effected in the nineteenth and twentieth centuries on the present situation in the West. In eighteenth-century Europe, there was a quite obvious contrast between the religious mentality of a fairly patriarchal group, and the secular mentality of the bourgoisie. The first revolution was a socio-political one (and hence socio-economical). In the second, the solidarity of men achieved through technical progress came to confront their exterior circumstances. The third revolution, spearheaded by psychoanalysis, was a personalist one: man came to see his interior condition, and he came to see that it was often at odds with his own free will.

In catechesis, therefore, it is necessary to know how a situation conditions man in his relationship with God. This also calls for subsequent reflection on the positive and negative aspects to be found in philosophical concepts of man. A deepening of faith in modern minds will normally presuppose critical reflection on an important aspect of anthropology, namely, that the person is a being in communion with others in the world and tends towards a state outside time.

Once this aspect of anthropology has been clearly grasped, the next thing is to recall the validity of distinguishing between the content (natural and supernatural) in God and the various cultural forms (myths, but not in the pejorative sense) which have succeeded in obscuring this content in God to some greater or lesser degree. Pope John XXIII pointed out this distinction in his inaugural address to the Second Vatican Council.

We will discuss the problem of man-in-situation, and how we can achieve a relative "demythologization" of our ideas about God—and in conjunction with this, how we can modernize what is valid in these myths—under four main headings.

1. GOD AND TECHNICAL PROGRESS IN THE WORLD

The progress in the positive sciences has done away with the mental image of an animist nature (though this is common in childhood and in primitive civilizations). Technological power has rendered prayer to "demiurges" useless. The lightning conductor has replaced the holy candle. But science and technology do not solve man's problems in the personalist order. For faith to be purified, a more accurate idea of the collaboration between God and human or natural forces, though without any suggestion of equality, is necessary. Man is made in "God's image," as the second-in-charge, the overseer of the world, and the collaborator in the propagation of life (Gen. 1, 27). Technological progress is a gift of God, who is the generator of the forces of nature and of human intelligence. There are many reasons why prayer should be especially thanksgiving on our part. Moreover, prayer helps us to make better use of technological progress.

2. GOD AND DISORDER IN THE WORLD

There is, on the one hand, natural catastrophe in the world which leaves man to a great extent helpless. There is often immorality which is never punished. There is virtue which is never rewarded. And on the other hand, there is a God who is silent, and who leaves the world to its own disorder.

These are real difficulties—they are not, that is to say, neces-

23

sarily petty. They do not, however, allow us to conclude that God does not exist or does not care; rather, they invite us to purify our ideas about God who is "living and active." Especially must we detach ourselves from our idea of God as a kind (or kinds, for circumstances vary) of demiurge, and grow in a new awareness of man's responsibilities. We must achieve a sense of the slow progression of the world in time, which conditions everything.

On the other side, there is a God who speaks and acts, but he always asks for conversion from us so that we may be better able to recognize and understand his word.

There is also a Christian meaning to suffering that we must come to know: that we must be faithful in the face of temptation, and faithful in charity in the service of our neighbor. There is profound joy and trust in the Christian life. We must be receptive always to the eschatological solution.

3. GOD AND DEPTH PSYCHOLOGY

When man examines his attitudes closely, and the sentiments from which they spring, he makes two discoveries which have a bearing on his belief in God. Negatively, these discoveries are as follows.

In the first place, he discovers that certain attitudes are the outcome of a stagnation in his psychological development, which usually took place either at the infantile or at the adolescent stage. This raises an important question: Is religion merely the stagnation of an attitude which has not sufficiently separated itself from the attitude of dependence which a small child has for his father?

Secondly, man comes to realize that fear and desire sometimes "create" their object. Thus man has created gods corresponding to his fears and desires. Science, furthermore, does away with the obscurity in which stagnation and illusions of the mind and imagination flourish.

Positively, on the other hand, these discoveries can be viewed thusly. In the first place, paradoxically, man can deny the negative approach in a positive way: anti-religious fears and desires create a *refusal* to admit the existence of God. Also, one should learn to profit from the progress made in psychoanalysis in order to make a sincere examination of one's ideas about God. It is possible for us to learn to realize that a certain personal deviation is mixed with a belief which is basically sound; the belief must therefore be purified from a myth which is only relative.

In the second place, it is important to distinguish between the different levels of fears and desires: between the superficial level of illusion, and the profound level where man discovers himself as he really is and with the utmost certainty. But then man discovers that his being exists in relationship to God. He realizes that God is drawing him on, that God resists his imperfect desires, that God is always asking him to transform his desires.

4. GOD AND THE PERSONALIST MEANING OF LIFE

Personalism stresses two values most of all: freedom and community in love. But that means that the relationships between these two values are conceived of from two different points of view. They are, of course, from the point of view of individual freedom, and from the point of view of fraternal charity.

Certain existentialists set up individual freedom as an absolute. In this case, another freedom can only be competitive and is an obstacle in the way of one's own freedom. Therefore, love is impossible.

Moreover, individual freedom does not exist in an absolute state, for it did not choose itself to be free. That is why life is absurd, for what really constitutes any meaning in life is rendered contradictory from the start.

25

To avoid this option of the absurd, and by opting for that principle according to which the real has meaning, the Christian personalist can only come to one conclusion: freedom is relative. It was created by God, it is real, but it is not absolute. Man has received freedom for the purpose of developing it by acting in concord with God's wishes.

Other authors of an existentialist outlook set up fraternal charity as an absolute. But this absolute is unrealizable and therefore unrealistic. Thus, since the absolute does not exist, there is no God. Or else they would place the absolute not in charity, but in man himself. To attain this absolute, man would have to meet God in an act of unconditional charity. But this is likewise unrealistic, and therefore God does not exist.

The solution to the first problem is this: The tendency in man towards a more and more perfect charity is not fully explicable in itself. The existence of charity is founded on the existence of God, who is its supreme goal and the source of its strength. As for the second, let us answer that man is actually not incapable of such charity, though he requires more-than-human strength in order to achieve it. This strength resides in a personal Being. God helps us by a gift in which we are collaborators.

1. COMMUNICATING THE MESSAGE

To communicate God's revelation and each of its manifold parts to man is the whole work of catechesis. This throws a preliminary light, therefore, on "how to do it": by not limiting oneself to treating of God in one section of catechesis, but by speaking about God all of the time, as a fundamental and continuous theme.

In many cases, it is important to preface catechesis properly so-called with an introduction. Pre-catechesis on the subject of God includes helping the catechized to become aware of human values as a necessary foundation of religious faith. This means helping him to acquire a sense of person, a sense of the sacred. This is something quite different from an apologetic approach.

The first rule of catechesis properly so-called flows from the primacy of the proclamation of existential signs over theoretical and practical explanations. God reveals himself above all in his actions, and therefore above all he shows these actions at work in events.

The kind of interpretation given to these actions, and its arrangement, will be adjusted according to the characteristics of the subject itself.

Preparation

The One in question is above both man and world, but he is present in both. This unity of transcendence and immanence lends itself to an arrangement of a dialectic type—the one aspect, then the other, but never one without the other.

Procedure

The "style" of the catechetical instruction will also profit from being to a certain degree "dialectic" when we are dealing with the transcendence and immanence of God. This procedure will show how, in spite of progress, our knowledge of God always remains incomplete while we are on earth.

The way to God begins by the mysterious call, "Leave your country." Man must leave whatever threatens to keep him imprisoned in "familiar" realities (at his own level or below him), and set out for what is beyond him. For the call, which contains an obligation, also inspires confidence; man sets out for the land where God is to be found. But this proximity to God, which is his goal, is already revealed from the beginning in the confidence it inspires. "I must leave myself to find God, but he gives me assurance that by leaving myself for him, I shall find myself again with him."

On the one hand, we must constantly remind ourselves that we can neither imagine God nor understand him adequately in a single thought or even in a series of complementary thoughts. Therefore, all comparisons and all formulated ideas must give place to deeper, more humble, and more progressive knowledge of him who is beyond us. On the other hand, we should not try to dispense with all imagination and all definite ideas, because our knowledge of God needs to be embodied in "mediations." These are truly valid when they lead to him whom they symbolize.

It is not enough that the procedure should unite the theoretical explanation with the practical application. It is also necessary that the catechetical dialogue show the relationship that exists between the catechized and God, and the commitment which necessarily follows from the true knowledge of God.

Our conclusion, then, bears on the goal and on the evaluation of method.

1. The object of faith is not the way in which God is expressed, but God himself, manifested in sign. This faith has several aspects: *Credo Deum*, that is, I believe that God exists; *Credo Deo*, I believe because I have confidence in the testimony that he bears (and which is manifested in sign); and *Credo in Deum*, I tend towards him, I respond to his call, I undertake to tend entirely to the final encounter in perfect communion.

2. "God alone speaks well of God." The primary meaning of this true statement is that all human words can only be very inadequate in speaking about God. This is why the words of the catechist are only a "mediation" of God who speaks. A second meaning is also valid: those who hear a man speak well of God recognize God speaking through that man. This is encouraging for the catechist, for to "speak well" does not here mean a human

gift of speaking, but a way of speaking which is faithful to God's revelation.

APPENDIX I: THE JUSTICE OF GOD

We know that there are several forms of human justice. Divine justice can be seen as a prolongation of human justice: God rewards the good and punishes the evil. God divides talents among men. There are signs of this justice in the Bible. Here the theme is continuity in justice.

But God is other, his justice is other than human justice. The recognition of this attribute of God asks of us a certain detachment from our human conceptions which we try to find on a larger scale in God, for example in our ideas on the proportion which should exist between work done and the ownership of the goods produced, or in our too simple egalitarian demands. Jesus came to reveal to us a more perfect justice of God. This is seen in the parable of the workers in the vineyard (Mt. 20, 1–16). But his message has been refused by many. Such refusal is a sin, and it gives rise to other sins also: when God does not answer our too human demands, we lose confidence in him, we envy other men, we even go so far as to blaspheme him. Christ, faithful to his message of divine justice, gives us the strength to be converted. Then we can understand better the justice of God. Here there is a theme of discontinuity in justice.

A theme of "going beyond" can be found in a third aspect of the justice of God. We must keep in mind that the biblical term "justice" signifies at once both more and less than our Western concept of it. The justice of God is the strength by which he establishes or reëstablishes men and things in the order which he determines according to his wisdom. This strength is penetrated through and through by his charity: that is why the justice of God gives more than any human merit can exact, and it is also the strength which pardons in giving life. The justice of God

29

is communicated to us by the Holy Spirit as a participation in the justice which Jesus received in his human nature. It helps us to be first "just" towards God, in love; and then to radiate this Christian mentality into all forms of human justice, especially social justice. But the total radiance and the plenitude of justice God promises to us only in the world to come. Our most perfect earthly justice is an anticipation of the eschatological justice. Through certain renunciations, our union with God and with men in Jesus Christ already goes further than the imperfections of human justice.

APPENDIX II: CREATION

In the catechesis of revelation, we must especially concentrate our attention on the preparation of the lesson. The data which we have assembled and selected in the course of preparation allow us to grasp the possibilities and requirements of the method to be adopted.

There must be reference to *facts*. In the case of the lesson on creation, the facts are established by the very existence of our fellow creatures and by our own existence, which we must conceive of in relation to God.

Secondly, there must be a grouping of *principal statements* on creation, from which a selection must be made.

What is the meaning, for example, of the phrase "to create"? Does it mean mainly to bring something out of nothing (negative aspect), or to bring a being into existence (positive aspect)?

"How" does God create? Does he create without need of materials or assistance (negative aspect), or solely by means of an expressed will (positive aspect)?

How are creatures, the created, to be viewed? As all that is not God, which is every thing? As especially man, "in the image of God"? In relation to Jesus Christ?

How are we to consider creation in relation to time: as its

beginning (initial creation), or as occurring at every moment (continuous creation)?

What is the aim of creation? Does God create for his own glory? Or for our own happiness? Or are the two aims the same?

What is the motive of creation? Charity?

What are the results of creation?

In the third place, the catechist must in his lesson explain the (anthropological) context of creation; this entails, needless to say, taking into consideration various modes of thought and different stresses on the doctrinal context. Thus in the case of the task which God the creator has allotted to man, there must be a moral stress: service which consists in observing the commandments; a stress on worship: praise expressed in prayer; an existential stress on inner-life: interpersonal communion (knowledge, love); and an existential stress on outer-life: collaboration in the task to be accomplished.

Or again, in the case of the expression "the image of God," there is both a Semitic context, which makes of the phrase a functional image: order and the propagation of life are thus insured; and a Greek context, which uses the phrase as a formal image: created spirit resembles the uncreated Spirit.

Another problem concerns the manner of conceiving of creation in its origins and in its extensions. Here there is both a static conception and a dynamic conception. The former views God as alone, who then brings beings into existence. Man is endowed with all qualities. It is a perfect creation. The dynamic concept sees God willing that living beings should subsequently complete themselves. Man awakens and develops towards personal and communal maturity. Creation must be perfected.

In the explanation of creation, furthermore, the literary context must also be taken into account, and the variety of literary styles should occasionally be underlined.

Finally, the terms which correspond to these different modes of thought and expression are consequently both numerous and

31

varied, and these must be employed carefully. If official catechisms mainly use notional and neutral terms (such as "God makes" or "God creates"), the catechist should attempt to complete these through the use of more personalistic terms, and in many cases these latter should even be given priority—God *summons* to life, God *gives* existence and strength.

The comparisons by means of which one attempts to illuminate an abstract statement in a more concrete way are equally of great importance in the context of modes of thought. As each one of these illuminates but a single aspect of truth, one must have recourse to several comparisons which are mutually complementary. For example, man works with the aid of materials, God works without materials; this is the source giving constant life to the river.

Finally, the catechist must attempt to go beyond any and all statements he makes about creation. He must not be satisfied with mere formulation whether it be concrete or abstract, but must proceed from the verbal sign (the notion or symbol) to the existential sign (living beings); and from the existential sign to the Person signified and active, God in action, in our midst, giving, summoning, assisting.

II

Jesus Christ

1. GOD'S WORD

How are we to present Jesus to the catechized? The answer, simply, is that we must in our catechesis present him as he presents himself.

But perhaps the word "simply" is actually too simplistic here, for on reflection we find that the question has been imperfectly worded. How, we should rather ask, can we make it possible for Jesus to present himself in our catechesis as he wishes to be presented? Jesus presented himself in a very kerygmatic manner in Palestine; and this is likewise the way that the Church has presented herself, since its origins, through the passing centuries, and in our own time.

By "kerygmatic manner" we mean the manner of the *"keryx,"* or herald, who proclaims a message, that is to say, the one who announces an event of special significance, and who claims therein a commitment from those who hear him. The whole mystery of salvation has the character of a message, calling each man at every moment to conversion as a means to communion. All catechesis (or proclamation and interpretation of God's word) must likewise be kerygmatic in manner. Didactic procedures (explanations given in the course of formal "teaching") and the active methods of pedagogy (research, discussion, and self-expression) will also have a role to fulfill, but it will be subordinate to the kerygmatic approach, which is the one most explicitly directed to the person-to-person relationship between God and man.

The Bible

God's revelation makes Jesus Christ known to us as the One in whom and by whom God accomplishes the mystery of salvation. The Bible shows us Jesus Christ as the living center of this salvation, which is an "economy" accomplished and revealed in a "history." The biblical outlook is, above all, "functional"; it is concerned with the significance of persons from the point of view of the function they fulfill, their precise function within the economy and the history. The very name "Christ" signifies an anointing for a function. We must know, therefore, who Jesus is "for" his Father and "for" us in the plan of salvation.

The Bible will also provide us with the necessary facts for knowing who Jesus is in himself, in his essence, but its purpose will be to show how this essence permits Jesus to fulfill perfectly the role entrusted to him in the plan of salvation. In the same way, the account given of the facts and their interpretation form the basis of a genuine history, but they are so presented as to make especially evident the saving mission of Christ.

The first proclamation made by the Church shows Christ in the light of his chief function, that of one who saves through action. It looks back to a time of preparation, and since the whole of the Gospel is written in the styles of thought and vocabulary of the Old Testament, we must also see how the history of the old covenant prepares the way for Christ.

We can see how Jesus, in the Gospels, presents himself in all his actions as the living "sign" of the revelation of salvation. His preaching—by deeds as well as by words (especially those deeds which were his miracles)—and above all his Pasch (that is, his death and resurrection followed by the mission of the Holy Spirit), make known to us the work of our salvation. These actions can lead us to the knowledge of his person and of his mission. St. John has said as much at the beginning of his Gospel.

The four evangelists include within their accounts of the progressive revelation of his mission, a description of the progressive revelation that Jesus makes of his person. This progressive revelation has its own kerygmatic dynamism, that is, at each step it makes an appeal to a more complete faith. It invites us, in fact, to a more perfect communion, one which requires a more perfect conversion. We discover this dynamism in the fundamental line of development which is in some measure common to all four evangelists.

This line of development can be detected in the "works" of Jesus and in his "hour." There is first of all a global presentation of his works: the kingdom of God has arrived. There is also an analytical presentation: because the kingdom is at hand, our values must become faultless, and we must acquire the disposition of perfect charity. Finally, these presentations are synthesized: the kingdom of God is in Christ and in the participation of all in his life (Jn. 6, 57; 11, 25; 16, 28; 17, 2).

The "hour" of Jesus centers mainly on the Eucharist, the cross, and on his glorified life.

This fundamental line of development, furthermore, has a double aspect: in a positive way, it stresses the accomplishment of God, namely, God's messianic gifts; and negatively, it stresses

Christ's opposition to evil, his struggle against sin, and the consequences of that struggle.

The connection between gifts of a messianic order (more perfect, but "other") and the struggle against misguided attachment to inferior gifts or to human "sufficiency," means that Jesus' invitation constitutes a continual appeal to conversion. The refusal to be converted leads to the tragical *dénouement* of the crisis, and the victory of fidelity over infidelity will transform this situation into salvation. St. Paul declares that the mystery of salvation is contained and summarized in the mystery of Christ (Eph. 1, 3–10; Col. 1, 25–27). We know about this salvation thanks to the light which radiates from the person of Christ (2 Cor. 4, 5–6). We share in this salvation according to our living "in Christ" (Eph. 2, 5; 2 Tim. 3, 12).

The Liturgy

The liturgy considers Christ to be, first and foremost, the mediator, through whom and with whom the Church offers to God her cult in spirit and in truth, and receives the divine gift. It teaches us, through the sacramental actions, to know God-made-man in the continuation of his saving action. The liturgy also gives visible expression to our adoration of Jesus Christ. By its prayers and instructions during the liturgical year, the liturgy presents to us the many different aspects of the mystery of Christ.

Life Witness

For the very reason that Christ truly acts in this world through the members of his mystical body, the witnesses of Christian living are equally "signs" by which he makes himself known. We can find the witness of some Christians in their writings and in their biographies. Men of art explain with particular brilliance how they see Christ. But every Christian who comes into contact with his neighbor in a Christian way is a "bringer" of Christ.

Reflection and Formulation

Doctrinal formulas elaborate three elements of the mystery of Christ: his incarnation, his redemption, and the Parousia. In our catechesis on Jesus, we must be very precise about our relations with Christ especially in these three aspects.

The central element of the mystery of Christ is the redemption. Jesus (Yahweh saves) is the One sent from God (he is the Son of man) as the perfect mediator. He has been invested with the salvific power of God. He snatches us from the power of the devil, in his victorious struggles against the assaults of evil, and he communicates to us the divine pardon (in the power to remit sins), as well as the divine life itself, a sharing in that which he received in his human nature.

By participating in our human condition, Jesus has assured for us a share in the redemption from that condition. This share itself depends on the help of God and receives from him its salvific value. Jesus reëstablishes mankind in its response to God, for its human condition is the consequence of a refusal to respond to God in charity. The first among men, Jesus does this in the name of all men; he does it by being faithful unto death, which the forces of evil inflict upon him. He thus offers reparation for our sins, and he receives the immortal plenitude of salvation in order that we might share in it.

In presenting redemption, we must be careful to avoid any apparent contrasts between the "angered" Father and the Son made man; it is, in fact, the merciful Father who gives us his Son. Another pitfall is to present Jesus as acting always "in our stead" in such a way as to make our listeners think that there is nothing left for us to do; in fact, Christ acts "in our name," and our solidarity with him is an active kind of solidarity. We should, therefore, rather insist on the way in which salvation takes place, first "in" Christ, and then "through" him as it comes to us. This is why it is so important to make clear the unity of the sacrifice on the cross and the resurrection (followed by the mission of the Holy Spirit). Thus it will be abundantly clear that we must receive our salvation from Christ, and that we must cooperate with Christ if this salvation is to "come to maturity."

As for the mystery of the incarnation, and its formulation, this may be considered from two points of view. First, it can be considered as the mystery of the person of Jesus, which is the foundation of the value of his actions. An essential analysis will make precise the notions of person, nature, knowledge and will, and so forth, in Jesus Christ. False problems should be avoided. A consideration springing from true wisdom will lead us more directly to accord to the prayer of Jesus its full value, especially to his contemplative prayer in which the Father gave him light concerning what he was expecting of him at different times in his life.

Or the incarnation can be considered as one of the several aspects of the function of Christ. Two aspects especially merit developed consideration: Christ manifesting himself, and the cosmic Christ.

Regarding the first, the incarnation may be understood as a mystery of the "manifestation" of God and of his action among us. The nativity of Jesus is only the first stage, for the manifestation of the active presence of God among us is much more striking in the death and resurrection of Jesus; and it will be completed only at the time of his Parousia. It is the whole life of Christ which belongs to the "mystery of the Temple," the visible and active presence of God among us.

Every manifestation of God is a call. It is not limited to arousing our adoration. It is always a call to a conversion of our mental outlook and an invitation to enter into a community of thought and action with God.

In relation to the cosmic Christ, the incarnation can be understood as a mystery of the sanctifying presence of God throughout the entire universe. In becoming incarnated, Christ sanctifies all that relates to man, and therefore the whole world of matter.

Considered in the perspective of a universe in evolution, furthermore, the incarnation is to be taken in an eschatological sense, and the emphasis is to be placed on continuity.

Similar considerations are at the basis of an "incarnational spirituality." This spirituality emphasizes the unity of the whole and continuity in sanctification. It sometimes neglects, however, elements of conversion, necessary at every moment because of sin, as well as what eschatology contains by way of discontinuity.

Finally, in our presentation of the mystery of the Parousia, we must show that the eschatological Christ is already present, but that our participation in him is always in progress.

Our relationships with Christ are based on the unity of Christ and his Church. The mystical Christ is a body of which Jesus is the Head and which all Christians are members of. It is a body whose unity does not repose in confusion (one acting in the place of another, or all acting indistinctly), but on interpersonal communion.

To attain a living knowledge of Jesus, it is necessary to meditate on his psychological and moral qualities. However, the presentation of our relationship with Christ can never be limited to these levels. The imitation of Jesus Christ must be the expression of our community of existence with him. Our relationship to Christ is fundamentally ontological, and in revealing it to us, Christ appeals to us for our response. He calls us to faith, which is a personal commitment to him. Deep-rooted from the very beginning, this commitment must become ever more complete.

Perhaps the best formulation is that so often used by St. Paul: "in Christ." We are incorporated into him. This fundamental reality throws light on the deep meaning of other aspects of the one reality. We are saved "by" him; we act "like" him, because grace makes us ontologically similar to him; we work "with" him, because men and the whole world must be made ever more Christian. We live as Christians in the measure that we "live in Christ."

Among the apologetical methods which can be followed to make the "guarantees" of Christ more explicit, the first choice should be that used by Christ himself: his person and his acts are marked by God's "seal."

2. THE HUMAN BACKGROUND

Psychology

Human dispositions, whether favorable or unfavorable to faith in Christ, vary according to each person's psychological evolution.

Little children are interested in Christ in that he works miracles and becomes the friend of the little ones. They admire his power and trust his ever present kindness. In our catechesis, we should draw attention to the real humanity of Christ: the growing Jesus is the child's model, and the adult Jesus has opened for us the way to heaven.

Older children give more attention to hard facts, and their memory can absorb explanations with ease. This period is therefore very suitable for speaking on the realities of the life of Jesus in Palestine, and for imparting a simplified doctrine of the redemption.

Pre-adolescents possess a certain ability to recognize links between different facts. They are interested in grand actions which demand courage and loyalty. They will therefore welcome the dramatic episodes of the Gospels: Jesus' fight against the powers of evil and untruthfulness, and his appeal to us to fight on his side.

During puberty it will become clear to the student that this fight is essentially an inner fight. In this situation, Christ becomes to adolescents the Lord who brings his power to help their frailty, and the understanding Leader who guides and supports their efforts to reach their ideal. We should be on our guard, however, against allowing them to stumble into the pitfall of closed introspection. The ideal can easily be presented as complete development of the personality. Jesus comes for the express purpose of breaking down the partitions of human self-sufficiency. He brings us life in divine charity. The chief problem in youth education is precisely the transition from an introspective approach to life, to an acting, open, and "social" approach. This is why adolescents should be told that union with Christ means an active union in his Church.

When the catechized have already acquired a more delicate approach to personal relations, and when they have discovered a deeper feeling of the mystery, it is the time to underline the two aspects of personal life in union with Christ. First, there is the "meeting" with Christ himself. That this meeting can become a very intimate and pure friendship with Jesus is not merely a question of affective experience, but above all of cooperation with him so that his grace may produce its fruits. Then, if this is understood, they must learn to become more christianly oriented, in view of their future task in the human community.

The interest of adults in Jesus Christ centers on the various problems and duties of everyday existence and on an acceptable vision of the meaning of life. It is in Christ that they must find the true and full meaning of existence, and the strength to work for the building of a better world.

Sociology

The manner in which one thinks of Christ and of his mission in life is subject also to the influence of the milieu.

In a Christian milieu we can sometimes come across two one-sided attitudes. On the one hand, in their doctrinal thought and in their sacramental attitude, some Christians do not take sufficient note of all the implications of the incarnation. Jesus has nothing like a human soul. Such Catholics never realize fully that on earth Jesus became one with humanity in the "fallen" state in which he found it, or that in heaven he has received, as "the firstborn" of a redeemed humanity, the total gift of salvation. Of course, grace was borne for us by Christ, but the vision of such Christians knows little about this grace being, for us, a participation in divine life (as this was communicated to the human nature of Christ). It considers the sacraments as the means and the present activity of the Son made man.

On the other hand, in their personal devotions and moral life, some Christians seem to forget that Christ is really God and that he is glorified even in his human nature. The memory of his birth and his passion attracts their tender sympathy and their affective compassion; before the Eucharist, they feel themselves moved to console him in his abandonment. They seek a support for their moral life in his human examples, and they consider him the most faithful companion in their work for the material and spiritual well being of humanity.

To avoid these onesided attitudes, catechesis proposes a synthetic view. But before examining how we might attain this end, we would like to point to the very radical results obtained by modern unbelievers in pushing the trend to consider Christ only as man to its furthest limits.

For these unbelievers, Christ is only a man of the past, though his influence is still felt; but it is an influence which can be called into question. These unbelievers pay homage to the sincerity and the nobility of Jesus' intentions and to the heroism of his efforts, and some of them even admit that he was united to God in a special way: there could have been "something divine" in him, especially in his charity, when this is considered in a pantheistic sense. But his attempt to make men live on a higher level has generally met with failure. His disciples found, in his example and in his words, support to live nobly and religiously, but this is an illusory ambition. It is an illusion with regrettable consequences for the social happiness of men, and so it must be remended. According to atheistic humanism, faith in Jesus Christ, the man-God who accomplishes our salvation, is a hindrance to the full development of man, to his liberty, and to his work in the world.

Whether we are dealing with believers or unbelievers, however, two traits of the modern mentality influence our manner of considering Jesus Christ. The first of these is the sense of the unity of the world, a unity which will be the result of universal evolution and the work of man in directing this evolution.

For the Marxist, it is a human work united to a better organization of society which makes possible the liberation of man in a better world on earth.

The Christian social movements seek to give to the struggle for better living conditions a Christian spirit, based on the example, the doctrine, and the grace of Christ.

The second trait is concerned with personal values, notably liberty and interpersonal community. The liberty of man is incarnated in the world, but it presupposes a transcendent discontinuity of man in relation to the it. Communion is on a much higher level than that of solidarity arising from instinctual or material interest; it requires the realization of the otherness of persons, and it is by the free gift of oneself that communal charity is realized.

The atheistic existentialists take into consideration the interior obstacles which man meets in the striving for personal liberty and communion.

Christians who, by thought and by action, serve these personal values, are grounded on the liberty of spirit which Christ obtained for us by delivering us from sin, which enslaved us and which made us oppose one another. These Christians put into action the strength of the Holy Spirit for a better communion of all men in the Church of Christ. This liberty and this communion, animated by grace, are both the source of the spiritual life which must become incarnate in all our activities, and the goal of this work of incarnation, the full stature of the total Christ.

To modern men (and especially to modern youth) who want to attain to fuller life, we must show that they should open themselves up to the true and acting Christ. It is in him and by him that their aspirations can be fulfilled, though in a "different way" than that usually put forward by merely human visions. Christ brings us the full life—as God has indeed planned it.

3. COMMUNICATING THE MESSAGE

In our presentation of Jesus Christ, our underlining of those characteristics which have a particular appeal to our listeners, should always be subordinate to the proclamation of all revelation in its coherent entirety and in its fundamental characteristics. Christ never makes himself known on a merely human plane. Neither is he a man who is searching for God in the company of his equals. Rather, he shows himself to be God's herald "par excellence," that is, he who makes the promised salvation a reality.

Preparation

The order suggested by this message of salvation places Christ in the center of all religious teaching. The best plan is to follow the unfolding of the mystery of salvation in history.

If we deal, during one year, with any one of the three classical subdivisions of the catechism, we can build up our subject matter on what we might call a "cathedral" plan. In the gateway, Christ appears in a "global" manner: he is the divine master who teaches the truths of faith; he is our Saviour, who gives us his divine life in the sacraments; he is our leader who leads and supports us in our moral conduct. An analytical explanation then attracts attention to the frescoes of the life of Jesus on earth. The synthesis finds its expression on the altar: it is through the eucharistic celebration that we unite ourselves to the really living Christ, in his sacrifice on the cross and in his resurrection, in order to practice fully the charity which he communicates to us. Finally, our whole orientation is always directed to the apse— where Christ is represented in the fulfillment of salvation.

The higher cycle of secondary education provides for a whole year consecrated to the study of Jesus Christ. The best plan to follow would be that of the Gospels.

Procedure

The manner in which Jesus Christ reveals himself is threefold: existential, dynamic, and personal. If we are to present Christ as he presents himself, then, how is our manner of presenting him to be based on these three characteristics?

1. Jesus makes himself known by his action in our existence. The Gospel signs of his existence are continued by the contemporary signs of his life in the Church. We must therefore show this unity—"*heri, hodie, et in saecula*"—incessantly. So, we must not take up any merely narrative presentation, based as it is almost exclusively on past events. Rather, we must present an action which is accomplished in history, and which is, notwithstanding, not limited to particular moments of time.

2. The signs of Jesus are called dynamic because they are an invitation not to stop at what is merely human, but to enter supernatural life. Therefore, in our catechesis we should emphasize how Jesus converts men: Nathanael, Magdalene, Peter, Paul, and each one of us. Moreover, we should approach these conversions from the point of view of the dispositions of each of these men, and of each of the students, as far as that is possible.

The Divine Master never loads men with more than they can

45

carry, but he never sides with their sins or their imperfections. Rather, he invites them continually to receive the light and the gift of God. This progressive presentation should be used also in our catechesis, especially in relation to the psychological, moral, and religious evolution of the catechized, and in relation to the growth of the imperfect Christian to a more perfect Christian life. In presenting Christ to young people, then, we should not try to "diminish" the supernatural dimension of his message to their own natural aspirations. It will only help young people if they can learn to integrate all their growing forces into an ever truer knowledge of Jesus. This warning is also valid in connection with the catechist's tendency overly to adapt himself to the varying characteristics of boys and girls.

3. The chief characteristic of the signs of Jesus consists in their link with his person. This means that our presentation should also be "personalist" in the deeper and truer meaning of this word. It should be a presentation which actually leads to the meeting with Christ. It should lead to a contact with him which grows into an intimate, loving knowledge, into a life of communion with Jesus Christ; and into collaboration for the salvation of all men. Therefore, we should show how Jesus comes to meet men, all and each, in a very personal way; how he meets and addresses himself to them personally; how he reveals to them, by the unity of his words and deeds, the love of God and the response to this love; how, finally, through our living communion with him, he makes us a share in the love which moves him.

The mystery of Jesus' person and his saving action shines before the eyes of faith—even if only through a veil which will not be taken away completely on this earth. Jesus is the Son of God, and he unites us to himself, and with him to the Father. In his divinity and in his humanity he is Son, who has received all from the Father, who lovingly accomplishes his Father's will, who, sent by the Father, completes the work of redemption. As a result of his sacrifice on the cross, we receive the gift of the Spirit, so that, even on earth, we can live in Christ and work with him for the continuation of salvation; so that, in charity, we can share in his glorious life for all eternity.

The entire presentation of the signs of Jesus is meant to stimulate the active faith of our listeners. We suggest that, at the conclusion of the presentation, the student give testimony to his living faith in a brief prayer—as, for example, in answer to the question, Lord Jesus, what do you mean to me? What should I be for you?

APPENDIX: THE HOLY SPIRIT

It is only for practical reasons that we are discussing the Holy Spirit, not in a full-length chapter, but as an appendix to the chapter on Jesus Christ, who sent the Spirit. We also hope to have it serve as a kind of transition to our discussion of the Church.

The sources for our catechesis on the Holy Spirit are mainly in the Old and New Testaments, and in the liturgy. In the Old Testament, the Spirit is not yet revealed as a Person distinct from the Father and the Son. There the word "Spirit" designates divine strength, and this appearance of strength is always apparent in his actions. The Spirit signifies the power and strength of God as opposed to the weakness of the creature. The breath of God is vivifying. He is the "divine wind" (Gen. 1). He makes certain men capable of pronouncing words and accomplishes acts surpassing mere human possibilities. It is the Spirit who "spoke through the prophets."

Jesus is filled with the Holy Spirit, and he acts under his interior motion. He reveals that he is "the Son," and he announces that he and the Father will send "Another" to act in the Church as an interior light and strength. The glorified Christ, finally, receives the fullness of the Spirit, and he communicates the Spirit to his Church (Acts 2, 33).

From the time of Pentecost, the Church is the Christian community living by the Spirit. The Spirit is the Pentecostal Fire.

In the liturgy, two attitudes towards the Spirit are especially apparent: one is that of supplication—*"Veni, Sancte Spiritus,"* and the other is that of adoration, common to the three divine Persons—*"in unitate Spiritus Sancti."*

Doctrinal reflection must help us to answer in a practical way two questions arising in connection with the theology of the Trinity: How can we take into account not only Western but also Eastern thought on the relationship between the three divine Persons? How can we understand the different "attributes" of the divine Persons, and what consequences must we draw from this differentiation?

However, before discussing from a practical point of view the differentiation of attitudes towards the three "different" divine Persons, we can show how our attitude towards the Holy Spirit will develop with regard to the characteristics of his actions. These are mainly to give divine strength to man (life on a higher level); to help him to interior action (transforming him in the depths of his being, in faith, hope, and charity, and by enlightening his Christian consciousness); by helping the Christian to radiate his faith, manifesting and spreading it in a universal way (witness); and by helping him to make a gift of himself in charity (encounter).

The study that catechists will devote to these questions requires completion in prayerful reflection on the role of the Holy Spirit in the very action of catechesis.

III

The Church

1. GOD'S WORD

The Bible

HOLY Scripture shows us how God realizes his plan of salvation by means of a community which continues to develop.

In the Old Testament, Israel, the chosen people of God, is called to the faith, eventually saved, and then blessed. Israel is wholly oriented to Christ, and it is from among this people that Jesus will be born; and this people must welcome Jesus with faith.

The characteristics of the Jewish people are concentrated in Christ, in a transcendental way. Through his actions—preaching, death, and resurrection, accompanied by the sending of the Holy Spirit—Christ gives birth to the Church, as the universal people of God, in which Christ himself prolongs his life. He also invests this community with the hierarchical and sacramental structure through which he continues his saving ministry.

The Church on earth, the mystical body of Christ, is "on the march" towards the final accomplishment of the salvation of all men. Especially important here is the testimony of the apostolic Christian community.

The complete kingdom, in the perfect people, will find its fulfillment at the end of time. This fulfillment is already realized in Mary, and the saints make up the glorious Church. Universal resurrection will take place at the time of the Parousia. Then all imperfections and institutional elements will disappear, and the Church, the community of Christ, will live perfectly forever in charity.

The Liturgy

The Church realizes and manifests herself in every liturgical action which she performs, but mainly in the Eucharist. Here the Church shows forth her aim, her nature, and her structure. Some of the Church's aspects are particularly manifested in the celebration of the Eucharist: the Church as a praying community, existing in order to honor God the Father, through Christ, in the force of the Holy Spirit; as a community which, in order to insure this prayer, is inspired by faith to listen to the word of God; as a community which unceasingly receives grace through sacramental signs; as a community whose prayer is hierarchically structured, and which realizes, through prayer, the union of all her members in charity. This prayer, further, is oriented towards the eschatological fulfillment, so that, in this prayer, the people of God acknowledge themselves to be "on the march."

Life Witness

The witness of the Christian life in the history of the Church and in our day especially, aids in a better understanding of the Church

50

more dynamic meaning when we note that the Church is unique by the very fact that she is catholic, that is, destined not so much to include all men, but to proclaim God to all men. Hence there is an apostolic task to which all Christians are called.

In those who are entrusted with Christ's powers, we recognize the dignity and efficacy of the function of the power, despite the possible defects of the person performing it. Concerning the role of the layman in the Church, therefore, let us first stress the fact that the layman lives "in the Church"; that he is, together with the bishops and the priests, a constituent member of the Church; that this is the reason why his primary role is spiritual and super-natural—notably in the practice of faith, hope, and charity, in prayer and in apostolate. What, then, is the function of the lay-man inasmuch as he lives "in the world"? It is that he has been entrusted with the temporal values—and not only he, but non-Christians as well. This is very significant. The layman's task, therefore, will consist mainly in penetrating his daily actions with Christian spirit, in giving, in all areas of his life, the testimony of a Christian life. Let us avoid in our catechesis giving the im-pression that the action of the Church—at least whatever action is properly her own—is the business of the clergy, and that the laity play a subsidiary role, as auxiliaries to the clergy. Rather, we must take this as our principle: Priests are at the service of Christ as his instruments, and they are at the service of the people, so that Christians may live in that charity which realizes the plan of God. The people, in turn, live in service to the world, so that all men may live in that charity which realizes the plan of God. The threefold ministry of Christ, therefore, can only succeed in full collaboration in charity between priests and laity.

We have spoken above of the spiritual and the temporal, but these terms are not quite exact. We see this more clearly when we compare the eschatological character of God's kingdom with its actual character, or compare the transcendence of grace with its immanence. The spiritual (that is, grace) is the value proper to

53

Christian life. The temporal is not just some kind of means; it has a real if relative value for the Christian, mainly insofar as it is related to the eschatological good. The fundamental law of the Pasch, following Christ's incarnation, death, and resurrection, calls for the implantation of, detachment from, and eventual transformation of the temporal values.

In this connection, in our catechesis distinguishing between objective and subjective holiness, let us never declare the ecclesial institution to be simply perfect, and the Christian's life to be simply imperfect. Rather, this distinction should lead to the discovery that the Church "on the march" is at one and the same time more than humanly perfect and yet subject to the imperfections of the world.

Finally, for it is apropos here, we would briefly like to consider the matter of the Church and apologetics. As soon as the Christian has reached the psychological age of reflection, he asks himself the question, Why am I a Christian? It is normal, of course, that a child born in Christian surroundings should participate ecclesiologically in the faith and life of the Church. But within this sociological conditioning it is his faith which must be developed. In the course of our reflective catechesis, therefore, the problem will arise of finding reasons which justify a Christian's continued membership in the Church. The Christian who is questioning himself about his membership will normally be very sensitive to the ministry and in the practice of Christian life that he sees about him. Apologetics must in no way wish to explain that everything which is said in the Church, even officially, or done in the Church, is the best of all possibilities. It is much more important that it make an attempt to find out what is the perfect truth or action, and to discover what the best corresponding practical attitudes are. Moreover, it must show that the Church "on the march" will always have defects—though the presentation of this aspect of the Church must never be done as an excuse for these defects. On the contrary, it is essential to stress the responsibility of each Christian to make constructive criticism, and to collaborate in the achievement of an ever renewed Church. In this connection, our catechesis ought thoroughly to examine the nature of the gift of charisma to individual members of the Church.

2. THE HUMAN BACKGROUND

The elements which allow for a correct appreciation of the Church are found especially amidst the element of a true community spirit, for Christian faith is especially communal consciousness and engagement. Those problems which arise as the result of the human condition, however, are not simply at the level of consciousness, whether of the right or wrong kind. They appear chiefly at the level of genuine integration of our consciousness of the Church being both perfect and imperfect.

Psychology

The Christian sense of community evolves according to a rhythm based on three fundamental stages: confusion, differentiation, and integration.

For the child, the community is mostly a human space in which he feels at home, where he feels safe. This is an instinctive solidarity, a feeling of "togetherness": in the family, in school, at play. Yet the child is aware that, while the Church is close at hand, it is also in some way universal. There is a slight element of confusion in his sense of community, therefore: his neighbors are next door, but he is told that they are also people he doesn't know.

The adolescent begins to differentiate. Negatively, he is opposed to any kind of forced participation, though positively he is making an attempt to free himself from isolation, and to enter into a common work undertaken for a better future. He is critical

55

of the faithful's mediocrity, of the way in which priests and religious live. He senses imperfections in the community. He has a radical thirst for what is best, and it is a radicalism without nuance and without patience. Our catechesis must help temper this radicalism by instilling social attitudes into this profound introspection. The adolescent must come to experience his own weaknesses, as a member in an imperfect community "on the march." Our catechesis must be flexible, making the Church neither too perfect nor too imperfect, but always making the adolescent feel that he is an integral part of the Church both imperfect and perfect. The result should be to loose him from a hypercritical attitude, yet not to deceive him into thinking that all criticism is invalid. He should be helped to realize that to have membership in the human community which is the Church, imperfect though it is, is the "most perfect" kind of communal membership of all, for its purpose is union with God.

The last stage, then, in the development of the sense of community, is one of integration—differentiation continues, but without opposition. In the true community, the personal element and the social element are both fully realized precisely through their mutual integration. The Christian, perfectly integrated in the Church, actively shares in her mission.

Sociology

In the general milieu of "the world," the Church has become a diasporic minority in a vast non-Christian world, and this world is becoming increasingly non-Christian on a technical level. Thus the Church is led, from a plane of "withoutness," to reflect on her task in the world. She must also constantly undergo an interior renewal under the inspiration of the Holy Spirit. She must be community-minded, preach the Gospel to the unevangelized, encourage the apostolate, practice ecumenism. These are the steps of the Church "on the march."

56

3. COMMUNICATING THE MESSAGE

The mystery of salvation is present in the Church visibly, actively, effectively, and, at the same time, in a veiled way. Our catechesis, therefore, must present the Church as an object of faith—that is, as the living Church, object of a living faith. Hence the required dispositions for this faith are not mainly on the level of sensible experience, of intellectual clearness or social efficacy, but on the level of openness to God and of superior knowledge and supernatural faith.

Preparation

The planning of our catechesis on the Church should be done according to the psychological development of the catechized. Special emphasis throughout, in addition, should be given to the Christian message seen in its entirety. We ought also to devote considerable time to the meaning of Pentecost in our lives. For older students, perhaps a year's course could be given to the presentation of the Church in action, on the call to participation.

Procedure

We should give special attention to those images of the Church which are present in the Bible, and which are taken up again in the liturgy. Part of the activity of the student could consist in determining how his personal life is now in union with Christ in his Church.

APPENDIX I: MARY

The Second Vatican Council, in its *Constitution on the Church*, has provided us with certain principles by which to direct our way of catechesis on Mary.

57

The first is that Mary has a special place in the Church; she is a member of the Church, but a supereminent and unique member (Chapter VIII, Article 53).

We know, too, that our manner of thinking of Mary at all times must always be within the context of the redemption (Articles 52, 54, 55).

Central to this fact is the teaching that there is only one mediator between God and man, and that is Jesus Christ. His mediation, however, does not exclude, but on the contrary constitutes the basis for, the participation of Mary's mediation, which in turn has its own unique character (Articles 60, 62).

A fourth principle is that all Marian doctrine must accord with ecclesial doctrine (Articles 63–65).

Also, the value of true devotion to Mary is that it can result in an "integrating affectivity," though one which always proceeds from truth and true faith (Articles 66–67).

Finally, there is an "eschatological dynamism" associated with Mary, for she "is the image and beginning of the Church as it is to be perfected in the world to come . . . a sign of sure hope and solace to the wandering People of God" (Article 68).

APPENDIX II: THE UNITY OF THE CHURCH

What revelation tells us about the unity of the Church can be considered from several different points of view. Because this is so, of course, different ideas of what this unity consists of come to the fore. As long as any one point of view is not exaggerated to the exclusion of other valuable aspects, however, it is legitimate.

There is a certain affinity between the four points of view on unity which we will now consider. We hope to show how each viewpoint, because of its relationship with a certain spiritual mentality, spontaneously accentuates a particular aspect of unity

—although, naturally, this aspect is not necessarily excluded from or even minor in the other points of view.

The Theoretical Point of View (with Practical Applications)

The presentation of such a viewpoint follows the inductive method, starting from various concrete manifestations of this unity in the visible structure of the Church and in the Gospels.

In his explanation, the catechist, because there are numerous meanings that can be attached to the word "unity," must now give a more precise definition of the subject. (If this were done at the very beginning, then the lesson would have begun in too abstract a manner.) There is, for example, numerical unity: there is only one Church which is the true Church; or unity of extension: namely, universality: the Church is destined for all men; or unity of likeness, particularly uniformity: the Church is one in her doctrine, since all believe in the same truths, and one in her cult, since all use the same sacramental means, and one in her discipline, since all obey the same authority.

The unity of coherence can also be chosen for presentation and explanation: the coherence of the Church is assured vertically by authority; Church life ought to be lived vertically in obedience, and horizontally in mutual charity.

The foundations of the unity of the Church are the will and the promise of Christ, and the fact that Christ founded the Church. The properties of this unity, furthermore, are two: in itself, the Church's unity is both interior and exterior, but also this uniformity is accompanied by certain differences. (A notional approach which emphasizes continuity often has considerable difficulty in explaining the legitimate differences in the Church, and is often tempted to reduce them to a kind of "subordinate uniformity": for example, a schism in the Church is impossible; the schismatic, who through lack of unity (of uniformity) is separated from the Church, ought simply to retrace his steps and *return* to the Church. Or another example: the unity of the Church does not experience any kind of evolution, because an "idea" does not evolve; it is merely the application of this idea which evolves.)

The application of the theoretical point of view in our Christian lives is necessarily derived from a kind of "overview" approach: we must all practice unity faithfully by confessing the same truths, by approaching the same sacraments, and by following the same directives emanating from authority. Moreover, we must pray for the return of schismatics and for the conversion of non-Christians.

The Practical Point of View (with Theoretical Motives)

If the catechist himself tends to think along theoretical lines, then the practical approach will consist mainly in emphasizing and developing the ideas to be applied in the theoretical point of view. The explanation, in addition, will be reduced to finding motives for that application: for example, in fostering zeal for the return of fallen-away Catholics to the unity of the Church.

The catechist, therefore, must first of all give practical examples of how men, women, and children pray and struggle for the unity of the Church. One begins with the example of the martyrs, who died for their fidelity to the unity of the Church (it is preferable that an English catechist give an example from English history, an American from American history, and so forth). Then he should describe the efforts made to convert the separated brethren, indicate the generosity and perseverance of the workers for unity, and also affirm the relatively poor results of these efforts, at least in appearance.

In the second step, the catechist ought to provide the reasons why we must all work for unity: because it is the will of Christ, as shown by various texts in the Gospels; because it is done for the salvation of the fallen away—certain measures must be taken (nuance is very important here); and because unity contributes to the greater glory of God, and is the call of the Church today.

As for the application, the catechist can encourage his students to pray together for reunion, and also urge them to widen their interest in this problem—through reading, or visits to reunion centers, or perhaps even set up seminars with students of other religious beliefs.

The Axiological Point of View

The purpose of this approach is to help the student reach fulfillment of his personality through contact with others, particularly with those who belong to the same kind of group as he does. The catechist, therefore, must first of all awaken in him the desire for unity or solidarity, then distinguish the orientations for approaching at this unity, and finally help the student choose which approach he will take.

In attempting to awaken a desire for unity in the student, the catechist must first describe this desire fully, that is to say, as it relates to both the human and religious levels.

There is in man a desire to form a unity with others in a homogeneous group. This desire is found at different levels: instinct finds in solidarity a means of defense and security, for both the individual and the group, but when reason is awakened, man then experiences the need for personal freedom. This experience sharpens the feeling for the legitimate differences existing between men. The personalist desire for unity, therefore, is the desire for the mutual relationships of persons, while respecting their differences. It is a pluralistic unity.

We could examine all kinds of manifestations (signs) of these aspects of unity, but then again, we must limit them, for example, to what concerns the psychology of adolescents, or of pre-adolescents, or of adults.

61

A manifestation of solidarity among adolescents would be simply in associating with adolescents of the same age level, and in exhibiting a common defense of their cultural life. A manifestation of freedom would be in group discussions in defense of their personal (common) point of view on life in general, or in common reaction against everything imposed from without or above. A manifestation of a desire for a pluralistic unity would be the interest which boys have for girls, and girls for boys, or for friendly competition with youths of other schools.

One can follow the same method in attempting to awaken the desire to suppress divisions. A manifestation of division on a grand scale (wearing clothes greatly at odds with general school and social standards) would be the resulting inconvenience.

After describing this desire, therefore, the catechist must now pose to his students the question of the (axiological) meaning which the unity of the Church has in this context. There are two parts to the question: What value has the Church in relation to the necessity for religious unity? What value has the Church for the promotion of unity in all kinds of human domains?

The religious unity which is proper to the Church and which has the greatest value for us can be considered according to various orientations, all of which have their advantages and disadvantages. Here we will attempt to determine which orientations have the least number of disadvantages, for their realization demands conditions which, taken together, involve a continual conversion to a better way of thinking and living as a Christian.

The first orientation is in considering the unity of the Church as an institution. Very organized authority assures uniformity. This is true above all in the case of the magisterium, which assures uniformity in the confession of (hence in the possession of) religious truth. Therefore, there is security in solidarity. This security comes to us through the Church instituted by Jesus Christ, and is supported by texts of the Gospels.

In order not to slip into the direction of disadvantageous consequences, we must grasp the role which our freedom has to play in its respect for the magisterium. In what concerns the essential elements of the content of faith, when the magisterium declares that these essential elements belong to the faith of the Church, the Christian freely enters into the uniform acceptance of faith, in union with the Church. But concerning those elements which have not yet been declared as belonging to the faith of the whole Church, and the different ways of approaching the content of the faith, the freedom of Christians is exercised in a legitimate pluralism. In both cases, the Christian has always the task of freely tending towards an ever richer and more profound life of faith.

This agreement with the unity of the faith of the Church can find itself faced with difficulties, in two ways. First, there can be conflict within a person's way of looking at the unity of the Church's faith. This matter can lead to prolonged discussion. Therefore, the catechist should either limit the subject to the immediate matter at hand, or put off to another lesson personal questions in regard to the faith; or he can reply by way of stating a principle. The solution to the problem can be found eventually in determining, on the one hand, exactly what truly belongs to the faith of the Church (for instance, it is not part of the body of faith that God created the world in six days and rested on the seventh), and on the other hand, in getting to the basis of the objection to the content of faith (the student, for example, may not know the difference between certitude which concerns purely objective data, independent of the intentions of people, and the certitude concerning the message to be met in the signs that one person gives to another).

Secondly, there can be conflict between fidelity to religious truths and the possession of other human values. A good example here is the life of St. Thomas More, who had to choose between fidelity to his faith (his personal conscience in submission to the authority of the pope was in accord with the faith of the Church)

63

and the possession of a political role, even of life. He became a Christian hero of fidelity to the unity of the Church.

Another orientation is in considering the Church as a community. The most living bond of unity consists in mutual charity. The most personalist value of that unity also resides there. It was precisely for that reason that Jesus came into the world, that he died and rose again. The Church is the community of all those who are united with Christ in the realization of the supernatural charity which is a gift of the Holy Spirit. St. Paul has elaborated this view in the whole of the Letter to the Ephesians.

This charity is identified with holiness. That is why it is so important to recognize the intrinsic connection between the properties "*una*" and "*sancta*." The Church is above all one because of supernatural charity, which constitutes its holiness; she is holy according to the measure in which she best exercises the unity of charity.

Supernatural unity is not visible of itself; it is manifested in the life of Jesus, as it is in his most striking signs. We *believe* in that charity, because Jesus lived it under our eyes and because he promised us his Spirit, who communicates it to us. But this supernatural charity contains in itself the need which we have for a living visible witness.

This witness must be lived in the liturgy—for the Eucharist is the sign of that unity, instituted by Christ, and made efficacious by his active presence, a sign of the love of Christians for God and for one another; and in daily life—the effective continuance of the gift of God, manifesting itself in all human actions, requires enduring patience and a humble perseverance.

That is the reason why it is possible that difficulties arise which militate against this mutual unity in the Church. In order to resolve them, each Christian ought, with the grace of God, to rid himself more and more of the interior obstacles which prevent him from thinking other than from his own point of view. An acceptance in charity requires a conversion both continuous and ever more total.

However, it is precisely the manifestations of this mutual unity, which descends more deeply and which rises higher than purely human sympathies, which constitute a sign of Jesus Christ in his Church: that is to say, the actions of the Holy Spirit.

An *heroic* example of this mutual unity was given in the course of the Second World War, when members of the French *Résistance* who celebrated the Eucharist on the eve of their execution, asked a German soldier to take part in the eucharistic celebration.

Finally, as we said, the catechist must help his students choose effectively and in an enlightened way which approach to unity he will take. This is to render operative the value of unity.

Let us take care, the catechist might warn, that our assessment of values and our appreciation of unity develop in the right same directions, for truth and charity live together in the unity of the Church and constitute the highest value.

Let us celebrate the holy Eucharist with more consciousness of what we are doing. Let us celebrate it more frequently, more actively, as the effective sign of the oneness of the community.

Lastly, let us radiate more, in our ordinary actions, the gift of the love of God, not only in our actions towards fellow Christians, but also towards non-Christians.

The Existential Point of View

The existential point of view approaches a situation as it has been or is being changed by new events. The central question here is, What is the present-day situation with regard to unity in the Church, and how should we contribute to its advancement?

Again, the catechesis of this point of view involves three steps for the catechist. He must first of all bring out the "signs" which are to be found in the present-day situation—that is, he must research. He must ask, Is there in present-day existential data a call from God?

This call can be in either the non-religious or the religious sphere. In the former, the catechist must research such forces at work as technical solidarity (in uniformity and interdependence) between men, and such material contacts as travel, radio, and television. These throw into relief the various resemblances and contrasts among the forces at work; they are polyvalent, that is, they either invite to mutual understanding, or provoke struggle.

He must also research, in the social area, those social structures no longer adopted or adapted (for example, total economic autocracy). He must also study those new social structures that have arisen, especially in the great urban centers, for which precise formulation is still lacking.

As for world events, the catechist must take into account such matters as the two world wars, space exploration (including the economic and cultural possibilities accessible here), writings which have opened new or wider perspectives for human achivement (those of Teilhard de Chardin, for instance), and so forth.

These are areas in the non-religious sphere. In the strictly religious sphere, the catechist should, for example, attempt to understand what impetus to unity the Second Vatican Council has given the world, even though, of course, at present he would be limited more to possibilities than to accomplished fact.

There are three questions which concern the unity of the Church. In light of this envisaged unity, are there any desirable modifications in the structure or other aspect of the Church which can help the unity intrinsic to the Catholic Church to manifest itself externally? Do any of these modifications concern the relationship between the Catholic Church and the other Christian Churches? Do any of these modifications concern the relationship between the Catholic Church and the secular world?

The basic principle to be followed in answering these questions can be formulated as follows: Without calling into question the unchanging "idea" derived from the "abstract" way of considering the reality, the position we wish to take up here is that of concrete consideration. The question then becomes: In what concrete consideration, in what existential manner, is the unity of the Church realized? The reply is: This unity is "given" by, or rather is a gift of, the Holy Spirit; from this gift it follows that we have a task to fulfill, in particular the task of working towards the increasing realization of this unity in the world. Through our own obtuseness, and above all through culpable negligence, it can happen that this unity is placed in a false situation. *In fact,* historically and in our own day, the universal unity of the Church exists in a developmental way (the Church is a church "on her way," or better, "on the march"). We can distinguish the way of progress (the apostolate, growth in the spiritual life) and the way of rupture (separation of individuals and of religious groups).

The structure of this development needs to be recognized and judged according to the existential sources of revelation.

The second step for the catechist is that he must interpret the signs of the situation, and indicate their significance. This latter, of course, is a matter of considered judgment. He must ask, What possible modifications are found in the authentic development of the history of salvation?

Here, too, a basic principle must first be understood. Some Catholics dread any change *within* the Church. Others, on the contrary, forget that the Church must preserve, through the centuries and throughout all history, unity-with-herself. It is necessary, therefore, to demonstrate that unity-in-diversity characterizes the whole *evolution* of the history of salvation, particularly as concerns the development of the people of God in their diversity.

The development of the Church is characterized by living tradition, which is to say that the same reality is transmitted in its essential reality, but that it is understood ever more richly and is expressed and presented in new (or rather, modified) forms. This

67

development is realized under a twofold influence: that of an inner principle of life (the Holy Spirit) who communicates light and love, in a way which finds expression particularly in the lives of certain saints; and that of cultural changes which provoke normal reactions (for instance, the dissolution of feudal empires).

The application of this principle to the present-day situation of the Church is best done with reference to what was done, and what is being written about what was done, at the Vatican council. In particular, the catechist can emphasize the "new" unity of ecclesiastical authority, noting that the primacy of the pope is permanent, but that it must now have a visible and operative link with the college of bishops. Or he may show the "new" unity of the liturgy, showing that while the essential elements of the Mass and the sacraments are retained, a re-new-ed form of celebration that takes into account the general characteristics of the present-day situation has been inaugurated. Here especially there is diversity in unity (the vernacular Mass is an excellent example of this).

Other applications could be concerned with the forms of religious life, with poverty, or with categories of thought; the possibilities are endless. The emphasis, however, is always on unity in multiplicity. A common mistake here is to overemphasize the multiplicity to the detriment of the unity.

We now come to the third and last step in catechesis from the existential point of view. We can formulate it this way: The catechist must help his students to collaborate in the kind of transformation which is suitable and called for.

What kinds of collaboration are possible? There is first the collaboration to promote a favorable atmosphere for unity. The paths which lead to it are the paths of ecumenism. Hence there must be collaboration in dialogue (this is not the same thing, we must keep in mind, as discussion); in a return to the sources of revelation (but not through a love of archaism) in order to understand it better and to think in a way more faithful to the spirit of the Bible and of the liturgy; in a reform of our own defects (exclusivism not based on the Gospels must be dispensed with); and in prayer in common, that we may all, Christians and non-Christians, together encounter the same living Christ, who communicated to us his Spirit that we may love all men, each man encountering Christ in the manner proper to him.

A second kind of collaboration is the working together towards the practical realization of unity in our own environment. We must work for this unity neither too hastily nor too tardily. On every practical point we must recognize and exploit all the possibilities which are opened to us. Here especially we should consult the conciliar *Decree on Ecumenism* and the *Declaration on the Relation of the Church to Non-Christian Religions* for guidelines. Essential reading here, of course, is the *Constitution on the Church.*

APPENDIX III: ECUMENISM

There are two ways of approaching the subject of ecumenism: either from the angle of continuity, or from the angle of discontinuity. This distinction, in turn, entails the following options in the way we may consider the Church. On the one hand, our catechesis can accent the uniform unity of the Church, her permanent and general institutions, her authority, her sacraments as an exercise of power. Or, the accent can be on the Church's "pluriform unity," on the varied (charismatic) gifts, on freedom in accordance with personal inspiration, on God's word and the sincere response in the interior attitude of the one praying. If we opt for the first approach, then we must stress what the Church has already received as redemption, as the inception of eternal life, as an efficacious institutional organization. If we opt for the second, then we must stress what remains imperfect in each man and within the whole history of mankind; we must accent the fact that the gift of God which is the Church is especially a promise of perfect salvation in eternity.

All of this is only to say that we must opt to accent either institution or event; either possession of truth completely revealed, and deliverance from sin considered as perfect in the instituted Church, although imperfect in the knowledge and effective charity of the members, —or the persistency of sin in Christians, the necessity of a growth in faith by an opening to all that the Lord wishes to say, when and as he wishes it.

We must view the Church either as the "already established community" into which those who do not yet belong must enter, and in which those who already belong must become ever more united; or as the "community to be realized in faith and charity."

We must opt to accent, finally, a unity of which the Church already possesses all the elements, and which is being realized in all those who put the established means into practice; and a unity which exists, or rather which is brought about, by the ever new and more complete gift of God, for which Christians must humbly beg.

IV

The Eucharist

1. GOD'S WORD

At the time of its origins, the paschal meal directly recalled the outgoing of the people of Israel from Egypt, although, as the history of salvation developed, it began to take on more meaning, until now the benedictions assume the whole of the events of salvation.

"We offer thanksgiving to you, O Lord, because you have given to our fathers a vast land, good and desirable, and because you have drawn us, Lord God, from the land of Egypt, and delivered us from the house of bondage; also for your covenant, with which you sealed our body . . ."

It is of the utmost importance to show what this meal signified at the time when Jesus took it with his disciples, when his "hour had come."

71

The Bible

1. THE FUNDAMENTAL APPROACH

In order to learn the full significance of the paschal meal in the history of salvation, we must look first at its preparation, and at the continuation of this preparation; and at its realization, and at the continuation of this realization. A simple diagram may help to bring all these themes out in better perspective.

Preparation	*Realization*
A covenant is made with the chosen people during their march to liberation, comprising outgoing, crossing, entrance. This covenant was sealed in blood in the sacrifice of communion and (later) also of purification. A memorial is instituted.	A covenant is made with all men in Christ during his "passage" through the world, death, and resurrection. This covenant was sealed in Christ's blood in the sacrifice of communion and purification. Christ institutes his memorial.
Continuation	*Continuation*
This memorial is to be reënacted until the arrival of the Messiah, in the paschal meal, in which each coming generation takes part in the old covenant.	This memorial is to be reënacted until the fulfillment of the Parousia, in the paschal meal, in which all mankind takes part in the new covenant.

The covenant is an expression of the fundamental reality of the "mystery of salvation"; it signifies the communion of mankind with the life of charity of God. The march signifies the profound meaning of our life on earth: it is an active crossing, owing to the power of God. We are freed from the land of bondage (sin), and cross with faithful confidence the land of trial, and finally enter the land of complete divine blessing. Half of the blood of the sacrifice is poured on the altar (the presence of God), and the other half on the people (see Ex. 24, 6–8). The blood is life; the union in the blood signifies the union in life, the vital union between God and mankind.

The memorial is a translation for the Hebrew word "*zikkarôn*" (Ex. 12, 14). Its active meaning is that "God continues to save his people and the people continue to show their acceptance of God." Thus there is a continuation of the divine initiative and of human collaboration.

The paschal meal was taken by the Israelite people before they set out for the deliverance from Egypt which the Exodus brought about. But from the time of the covenant, it became also a meal of communion; and because the people were in possession of their land, it was a feast of gratitude, celebrated under peaceful circumstances.

However, the people's infidelity had made the covenant precarious, but then the prophets announced that a new covenant would be made, by the Messiah. For this reason, the paschal meal took on the significance of a messianic and eschatological expectation. Even now the Jews still pour out a cup for "Elijah, who is to return," and they leave the door of the room open for him as an expression of their hope.

During the Last Supper, Jesus carried out the promise made by the prophets and transformed the Jewish meal into the Christian meal of the new covenant. The account given by the Gospels stresses both the continuity and the novelty of this meal. This transformation, moreover, succeeded in synthesizing two modifications of signification: 1) the new covenant is more perfect than that of Sinai because it is *more* spiritual (see Jer. 31). Jesus' blood put the seal on this covenant, which is a *more* perfect communion between God and man. The meal instituted by him makes men sharers in the sacrifice of a *more* perfect communion.

73

2) The new covenant redeems man by delivering him from sin. Jesus' blood poured out for the remission of sins resembles the sacrifices of expiation, but its power to purify was *greater*.

This change in the significance and value of the meal is accompanied by an appropriate change of sign: the material sign is no longer the lamb of a nation of shepherds, but bread, the food of all men; the verbal sign reveals the double significance of Jesus' blood: the sacrifice of covenant and the sacrifice of purification.

The paschal meal thus transformed was instituted as a memorial to Jesus-in-the-conclusion of his covenant. Just as Moses had instituted a *zikkarôn* of the first deliverance, Jesus declares, speaking of the new meal, "This is meal *zikkarôn*." These words, translated as "Do this in memory of me," are to be understood in the complete context of the new and redeeming covenant, to which is entrusted the "memorial" of Jesus' active presence and participation.

2. THE ANALYTICAL APPROACH

Our discussion here centers on the concept of sacrifice. In the New Testament, the meaning and forms of sacrifice are to be interpreted in the context of the sacrifices of the Old Testament. Moreover, it is important to take into account the evolution which took place during the centuries of preparation, as well as the transformation which the sacrifices of the Old Testament underwent in the New, and this under three forms: the cross, heaven, and the Eucharist.

In order fully to appreciate the context of the Christian sacrifice, we must first know the stages of sacrifice which led up to, or rather, prepared for it. At the time of undeveloped Jewish civilization, nomad at first, the meaning of sacrifice corresponded to a fundamental, valid, innate tendency on the part of man, though in the forms of sacrifice divergent tendencies were also manifest—for example, in the tendency to "get even" with God. The rite replaced heart.

The purification of sacrifice was preached by the prophets, who stressed the importance of the heart, or "spiritual" sacrifice. They distinguished between ritual and lived (existential) sacrifice, but also united the two.

The third stage was the transformation of sacrifice accomplished by Jesus Christ. His acceptance of his "hour" (cross and resurrection) was not a ritual but an existential sacrifice. However, the meaning of his acceptance can also be expressed in ritual terminology, though in a sublimated (that is, analogical) way.

The eucharistic sacrifice is now celebrated by Christians. It is existential in that it relives Christ's sacrifice in view of the Church's participation in the offering act and in its effects. It is ritual insofar as this reliving is done within a rite, and involves the ritual participation of the faithful, though it has as its aim an existential participation.

The three stages of sacrifice likewise correspond to three aspects of sacrifice, and again, though each has its proper form, they frequently overlap and blend together.

There is, then, first of all sacrifice of praise. This consists of tribute, gifts in honor of God. As far as this aspect concerns the eucharistic sacrifice, we must keep in mind that Jesus is not a kind of "wealth of which one deprives himself," nor is he a "gift." Here the catechist must stress the inner dispositions of obedience and love.

Secondly, there is sacrifice of expiation or atonement, of purification, of propitiation. In the Old Testament, this sacrifice was symbolized by the sprinkling of blood, which was considered an "instrument" given by God so that the priest could perform the ceremony of purification (see Lev. 17, 11).

In his catechesis on this aspect of sacrifice, the catechist should stress what God expects of man, the inward disposition; to turn aside from an attitude of refusal; to ask for pardon; to open one's heart to the "gift" of God.

The application of this aspect to the New Testament, furthermore, is a more delicate matter than one may perhaps suppose. We must in our catechesis insist not on the fact of our offering the expiation of Jesus in place of our own, but, on the contrary, we must emphasize the call to join our inward dispositions and the actions by which they become incarnate, to the sacrifice of propitiation of Jesus Christ.

There is also the aspect of communion. In general, this kind of sacrifice involves manducation—thus, especially, manducation of the paschal lamb. (There is no question, however, of a purifying of sin by blood.) The main sacrifice of communion is that in which the covenant is sealed: half of the blood is poured on the altar, half on the people.

Christ is the paschal Lamb of the new people of God. It is in the blood of Jesus that the new covenant was sealed. This covenant is realized by Jesus' "paschal" death which is a passage towards the Father. The glorious life is an integral part of the total sacrifice.

The eucharistic sacrifice has a twofold aspect. It is in the first place a community meal with the risen Christ, an anticipated eschatological banquet. It is also a sustenance for the Church on her way amid earthly imperfections, a source of strength, yet a feast for sinners.

In our catechesis we must show how the community meal is the fruit of the sacrifice of communion, and how this fruit and this sacrifice affect our union with God. God enters into communion, moreover, with each person who is a member of the "new alliance," so that the sacrament of communion with God is also the sacrament of communion between men in Jesus Christ. This sacrament is the "sign of charity," and Christian fraternal charity is its special fruit.

We must also insist on the necessary preparation in order not to profane a sacred feast, yet on the other hand we must make it clear that this feast is also meant to provide strength to men in their imperfection.

Finally, we must emphasize the necessity of confiding in the grace of God that will be given at this feast, which has been prepared for us by the Lord himself.

There is in the eucharistic sacrifice a real and active presence of the paschal Lord. Real presence is not some kind of "thing": the glorious Christ is *present.* He is present not for the purpose of filling a physical or earthly void; rather, his presence is directed to the active continuation of the mystery of salvation. Jesus who is present acts within us and uses our activity, enlightened by his Spirit, to act in the world.

Therefore, let us not stress any kind of "solitude" of Jesus in the tabernacle. What must be made evident is that the eucharistic sacrifice is the prolonged and repeated meeting with the One who continually operates within us and throughout the world.

The Eucharist, to sum up, should be presented as the principal celebration of the redemption, the liturgical participation in Christ's "passage"—which is the "existential way" of Christ dead and risen. It is a participation which increases charity between all those who live in communion with the Father, the Son, and the Spirit.

The Liturgy

The basic structure and significance of the liturgy of the Mass are to be understood, first of all, within the context of the Jewish liturgy, from which the Christian liturgy is derived. We find in the Jewish liturgy the framework of the paschal meal, though now transcended, the liturgy of the sacrifice of purification having been integrated into it. The Jewish liturgy also provides for the framework of the liturgy of the word such as it was celebrated in the synagogue.

The structure of the liturgical action is threefold: the introduction; the liturgy of the word, consisting of proclamation and the acceptance of the word of God in faith; and the liturgy of the Eucharist, consisting of preparation, oblation, and completion.

The liturgy of the holy Eucharist being the development of that which Jesus willed when he said, "Do this in memory of me," it is of the utmost importance that, in our catechesis, we heighten, as our first step, the identity of the fundamental structure that lies between the Last Supper and the sacrifice of the Mass.

To this end, it would be preferable to begin our catechesis with the center of the eucharistic liturgy, namely, the consecration, and especially with the beginning of the consecration, that is, the preface, which is not an introduction to the eucharistic prayer, but precisely the solemn outset of the great prayer which goes up to the solemn doxology and reaches the *berakâh* of the Jewish liturgy. It is a great prayer of praise.

It is hereby that the vertical dimension of the Last Supper is found in the Mass. In the middle of the consecration is situated the prayer of consecration, which is the oblation of the sacrifice. So far as the active participation of the faithful is concerned, the aspect which one might prefer to emphasize is that of the engagement with Christ in his rising towards the Father.

This rising is fully accomplished during communion. Here we participate in the "completed union" established between Christ risen from the dead and his heavenly Father.

The celebration of the memorial of the deliverance and of the covenant also has a horizontal dimension, for the Israelites had become a privileged nation, precisely because they were divinely chosen by God (saved by him and welcomed into his covenant). This also happens for Christians in the consecration and in the communion of Mass. The dimension of charity was manifested in the fraternal feasts taken over by the Christians. However, experience soon proved that calling together fostered attitudes contrary to Christian charity; and rather than a real worship, the meal became instead a profanation (1 Cor. 11, 20–29). In order to avoid further deviations, the Church transformed this ceremony into a rite which constituted a performance for the faithful, bringing the gifts destined to the community who came to celebrate the Eucharist. A certain share of the gifts was put aside for the sustenance of the clergy and the poor. Thus, in linking the horizontal aspect of fraternal charity with the vertical aspect of the cult rendered unto God in Jesus Christ, the offertory has become a gesture of the faithful towards the priest, and also a prayer offered by the priest over the gifts brought by the faithful. It is a way for the latter to express their desire to be united in the sacrifice of the Lord, which will take place at the consecration-communion when the priest destines the bread and wine to be changed into the body and blood of Christ.

The liturgy of the sacrificial meal having been thus elucidated, the catechist might now show how the liturgy of the word fits in at the present time. This liturgy proclaims God's initiative in inviting us to partake at the banquet of the alliance. Up until the time of the fourth century, the celebration began with the reading of holy Scripture (as it is read on Good Friday).

We give our answer in union with Jesus at the consecration. God the Father effectively communicated to us the gift of charity in a more perfect manner in holy communion.

Life Witness

The communal celebration of the eucharistic sacrifice is the witness par excellence of our Christian life. Our catechesis on the Eucharist from the point of view of witness, therefore, is in many respects our catechesis from the point of view of Scripture and especially liturgy. A problem which may arise, however, concerns the effective and operative integration of liturgical community with social community. In other words, are Christians a community before they gather to share the bread of Christ, or does this gathering in effect "make" of them a community? Men are social by nature, but there is a dividing element, namely, sin. In our catechesis, therefore, we should stress that one of the requisites for an effective liturgical community is a witnessing social community. Liturgical community is social community realized in the fraternal charity of Christ.

Reflection and Formulation

The eucharistic sacrifice is an action which unites us with God. It is, then, an interior act expressing and realizing itself in an external sign.

It is an interior act in that it involves the gift of self in obedience —and in that, in order for this gift of self to be possible, we must renounce all that impedes our union with God. "I offer myself," which is to say, I renounce all that keeps me far from God. I place all my powers at his service. I will do all that he wills of me. I will place my happiness in him, especially in being intimately and eternally united with him, in participating in his life of charity.

The eucharistic sacrifice is an exterior sign because it is not sufficient that man merely express this wish to be united with God. Only God can enable man to be admitted to the divine domain, to be sacred. God gives his priest the power to sanctify, which is to sacrifice "efficaciously."

In the realization of the eucharistic sacrifice, both in an interior and exterior way, there are two essential components: a rising to God, which is oblation; and accomplishment, which is union with him.

Jesus has stated clearly in what way and in which sense we must realize his sacrifice (see Jn. 17, 19ff.). Through his death, Jesus returns to his Father in order to be more perfectly united to him in his glorious humanity, and in order to enable men to be integrated into this union.

Jesus' sacrifice consists in his return to the Father by the way which the Father traces out: through gift of self in obedience, in his role of redeemer who offers reparation for our sins. The sacrifice takes in his death and glorification, his oblation and accomplishment.

In heaven, Christ lives eternally in the gift of self to the Father and in the welcome of the gift which the Father extends to him.

The Mass is a real sacrifice, therefore, but it is also a relative sacrifice. The gift of self, which Christ has expressed on the cross through his death, and which he makes eternally, is made present (by him) among us during the rite of consecration. This rite, introduced in the prayer of the Church, is at the same time the efficient sign of the union of the sacrifice of the Church with the sacrifice of Christ. Christ offers himself, we offer Christ, we offer ourselves, he offers us.

Our sacrifice consists in our active participation in the sacrifice of Christ. Our baptismal character renders us capable of "participating efficaciously" in the liturgical celebration. We do it by corresponding to grace, by conforming our interior dispositions to those of Christ, and by taking an active part in the eucharistic celebration.

To participate in the Mass, therefore, is to accept and realize the paschal meaning of our life, that is, by triumphing over sin, by growing towards the fulfillment of charity, by "ascending" with Christ towards the Father, who communicates his Spirit of charity to all the members of the Christian community.*

* The link existing between the redemption and the Eucharist, as they are both seen in a paschal perspective, is brought out in the *Constitution on the Sacred Liturgy*, especially in Articles 5, 6, 7, and 47. The text of Article 47 uses for the most part the formulation of the Council of Trent. It recalls the institution especially in reference to the sacrifice of the cross, but quite remarkably it does not use the term *"repraesentaretur."* It does not once use the word "renew." Similar expressions, against which there are some very considerable arguments, are already very widespread, but they are used outside official texts. The *Constitution,* instead, selects the word *"perpetuaret."*

81

2. THE HUMAN BACKGROUND

There are elements both favorable and unfavorable to the degree of sensitivity which we will have towards the Eucharist, in all its aspects. This is true both of the contents and the forms of expression of this sacrament.

Psychology

There corresponds to whatever aspect of the Eucharist which we choose to accentuate, a spirituality which can be developed and transformed in light of the mystery of salvation. The most valid of these spiritualities, we believe, is that which synthesizes four aspects of the Eucharist, which is to say, four "spiritualities," namely, eschatology, the cross, the incarnation, and redemption. Moreover, as we have elsewhere made clear, there is a certain analogy between these aspect-spiritualities and the evolution of psychological ages.

However, all spirituality must eventually become "adult" spirituality, for Christ is the center and nourishment of all Christian life. The catechist, therefore, in his catechesis on the Eucharist to the various age groups, should attempt to synthesize those spiritual aspects in eschatology, the cross, the incarnation, and the redemption, and attempt to relate them always to the Eu-

---

"Making this sacrifice actively permanent" means continuing this sacrifice in a way which is suitable for the present situation. The manner in which this is done is indicated by the reinterpretation, also very remarkable, given in the following quotation from the text: "At the Last Supper, on the night when he was betrayed, our Saviour instituted the eucharistic sacrifice of his body and blood. He did this *in order* to perpetuate the sacrifice of the cross throughout the centuries until he should come again, and so *entrust to his beloved spouse, the Church,* a memorial of his death and resurrection . . ." Once more, mention of the resurrection has been added. Also, the eucharistic celebration is described in several other ways, among which we note especially the phrase "paschal meal." The *Constitution* cites the time-honored "*O Sacrum Convivium, in quo. . . ,*" but it replaces very significantly the phrase "sacred meal" by the phrase "paschal meal."

charist, for it is in the Eucharist that our work of redemption is being carried out.

Sociology

As to the forms of expression which the eucharistic celebration of our redemption assumes, these will be more or less well "understood" by the student first according to how responsive and active he is in the eucharistic celebration itself, and secondly, according to the historical and sociological environments in which this worship takes place.

If, therefore, we always keep the paschal reality central in our catechesis, we can then go on to underline its various aspects from the point of view of age and milieu. We can formulate these aspects thus, progressing from catechesis to children to catechesis to adults.

The Eucharist is our prayer with Jesus among us, with Jesus who would lead us to the Father. We must promise never to let go of his hand, when the road he shows to us becomes difficult. We must ask to be with him always.

We are invited to come and receive the living Bread, Jesus, who gave us his life, so that we may follow in his footsteps and grow as true Christians.

We must pray with the Christian assembly, in a repast of charity. There we receive Christ's grace to practice fraternal charity.

We must respond to all that God expects of us, after baptism —when we entered the Church of Jesus Christ. We must commit ourselves to being faithful to him, rendering glory to God and working for the salvation of all men.

We must associate ourselves with the whole Church to the sacrifice of the cross, accomplished in heaven. Jesus has returned to his Father and lives with him. We take part in his sacrifice, rendered present on the altar by Jesus.

We must find in union with Christ the power to conquer our difficulties and to live a truly beautiful life.

We must walk with Christ on the great road leading towards the promised land.

We must give ourselves to God, in active union with the sacrifice of Christ.

We must live, in its most intimate aspect, the central event of the redemption—the mystery of salvation—which includes the contents of our faith, the essence of our life as a Christian.

We must act as a "man before God," by recognizing his sovereignty and kindness, by public acts of homage. As "man and sinner," we must make reparation. As "man called by God," we must welcome the divine gift, respond to it, be filled by it.

We must try to make our whole life reach its highest value, union in Christ, by synthesizing in ourselves the value of oblation—participation in Christ's sacrifice; the value of conversion—detachment from our anthropocentric attitudes; and the value of superanimation—by putting charity into all our actions.

This participation in Christ's Pasch is already the reason for our deepest happiness here on earth. It gives us the courage to go forward to the final goal. It is a preparation for the perfect union in eternity.

3. COMMUNICATING THE MESSAGE

Preparation

Our preparation should be threefold: we should determine the meaning of the Eucharist in the history of salvation, especially in the two testaments; we can then go on to show how the eucharistic celebration was developed in the Church, along the main lines of today's celebration; and finally, we can give a doctrinal-moral explanation of the important aspects of the Mass —that is, the sacrifice (cross, heaven, altar); the act of Christ and of the Church; the fruits of communion; and veneration of the real presence. Our preparation should also include, of course, a liturgical explanation of the ceremonies, and how the students can take an active part in the celebration, but this presentation should come last of all.

Procedure

There are four styles, so to speak, which we can adopt in our catechesis, though in fact they are four parts of a catechetical synthesis.

The first is the personal. Here we must avoid "reducing the matter" either to the offering (a present) or to a communion. Sacrifice is the gift of self in love. The meal also includes union between persons in conversation. The eucharistic meal is a prayer. It is "interiorization" in recollection.

We must also catechize from the point of view of community spirit. We must insist on the union of man and God in charity; on the necessary dispositions for this charity; on how this charity is expressed in the celebration, how it radiates in all our actions.

Thirdly, there is what we might call "strictly true" catechesis. The Mass is a sacrifice unique of its kind; it is related to the sacrifice of the cross, which is also unique of its kind. We must therefore never use expressions which suggest a kind of "historical renewal" of the cross. During the Mass, the sacrifice of the cross is present in its glorious phase. Moreover, we must never try to demonstrate the unity between Mass and cross by the use of superficial comparisons and images. We must appeal, rather, to faith, which recognizes the mystery of an identical gift expressed in two different ways. We must respect the role proper to Christ, the role proper to the priest, and also the role proper to the faithful, according to the meaning which we give to the phrase "offer holy Mass."

Finally, there can be a dynamic style of catechesis on the

Eucharist. This means that we must never linger on juridical aspects, or on those inspired by obligations arising from positive law, or on those of a "work" which will be rewarded. We must present the Eucharist in an atmosphere of generosity, as a noble duty arising from our dignity as Christians, as a joy. The Mass is the full recognition of the gift of God. We must "utilize" our "best talent," which is love, in celebrating the Mass. The Mass is the most "active" union we can have with Christ, in faith, hope, and charity. It is the most fruitful sharing of the Pasch of the Lord.

V

Morality

1. GOD'S WORD

The Bible

WHEN God made known to Abraham what he expected of him, he did not present him with a code of laws; he did not speak to him of human progress; he did not tell him that he was calling him to the intimacy of communion. He simply exacted of him a basic attitude of faith, in virtue of which the patriarch set out on the way which would lead him to his goal. The three dimensions of God's word—the objective, subjective, and interpersonal—were, therefore, still indistinct, but already the global presentation was marked with a personalist and religious character.

In the course of Israel's history, the dimensions became more and more distinct, and a certain overlapping took place which threw the normal tensions out of balance. The Mosaic law provided a positive conditioning for a personalist covenant. Soon after, however, the legal and institutional aspect of the Law, especially as it concerned the liturgy, tended to become identified purely and simply with the response which man makes to God and from which he hopes to garner his "religious security."

Eventually, the prophets reacted and stressed the supreme importance of moral dispositions properly so called, that is, interior attitudes to be put into practice with the very strength which the God of the covenant gives for this purpose. They promised that the divine activity would work on man's heart to transform it and to help it act in accordance with this interior law of communion with God. The other aspect of human development, namely, the aspect expressed in a morality of values, is found only implicitly in the Scriptures, for the Semitic mind did not consider values in an explicit way as factors in the development of man's subjectivity, but rather as tasks objectively entrusted to man by God. The nearest approach in the Bible to what would later be called humanism is "wisdom." Wisdom is first of all conceived of as the knowledge (and putting into practice) of ways of behavior for succeeding in life, or for "finding a reason" for inevitable failure. But this human wisdom was opposed to God's views. This is seen in the conflict between the prophets and the political advisers to the kings. The preference given to short-sighted human views led to ruin. Israel in exile is converted, especially those among the people who rally to God's views and who thus participate in divine wisdom.

After the Exile, a divergence between two "moral" attitudes became apparent. On the one hand, the influence of the rabbis gave weight to the legal concept in Pharisaical circles; it introduced the "sufficiency" of the man who trusts in his works as conforming to institutions. This was a closed, static morality. On the other hand, God's action increased a truly interpersonal attitude in the hearts of the "poor," that is, those who did not side with so-called human strength (or with money, power, works which conformed to the Law), but who trusted in God to guide them and sustain them in all circumstances according to the unforeseeable invitations of his love. This was an open, dynamic morality.

The history of the Old Testament is one of a long ripening of the sense of moral obligations and the unfolding of what they contain. There is to be found also the attitude of those who insisted on remaining fixed in the past with all the narrowness, yet with all the temporary license, that this implies, and the attitude of those who were ready to accept progress in moral concepts and the institutions incorporating them.

Jesus Christ brings us complete revelation concerning what degree of tension ought to exist between the different aspects of the response God expects from man and the content of this response. Jesus, in fact, reveals to us God's will in the first place and above all by making a response-in-acts to his Father's call, that is, not by simply practicing precepts, but by living as God wills man to live, interiorly and exteriorly, in the light and under the impulse of the Spirit of God. Thus, all of Jesus' actions emanated from charity and constituted "incarnations" of charity, which is the love of God and the love of man.

Concerning preaching as a means of revelation, Jesus linked up his words with his acts, and his acts with the permanent activity of God in the history of his people.

Faced with the divergence existing between the Pharisees and the "poor," Jesus took a firm stand against all the defects of legalism: rigidity, sclerosis, sufficiency. He ranged himself with the prophets and recalled the necessity for interior dispositions, and he declared that it was the "poor" who were united to God in his kingdom. This does not mean that he was suppressing all law; on the contrary, he referred explicitly to the commandments of God. He replaced certain prescriptions of the Jewish law with Christian institutions, and he instituted a hierarchy which would also have to promulgate laws so as to give a permanent or transitory clarification of the exigencies of the Christian life.

The insistence on interior dispositions in the Gospel makes it possible to find a morality of Christian virtues and, in this sense, a Christian plan of human progress in the service of God. We know that, especially since the Exile, perfection for the man of the Bible consisted in access to the wisdom of God. Several of the Johannine discourses of Jesus are based on the invitations of Wisdom to partake of his banquet. Man's perfection is his "knowledge of God." The oft-quoted words of St. Irenaeus, "God's glory is man's life," are completed by the same Father of the Church with the following sentence: "Man's life is the vision of God." The knowledge which is spoken of here, however, is the experience of communion with God, and the perfection of this experience presupposes the adult development of one's life within the human community. This is charity, and it brings us back to what is essential in the morality of Jesus.

Charity finds its synthesis in an active response to the imperative call, "Follow me." This means that to imitate Jesus morally in one's conduct presupposes a psychological contact on the part of Jesus and the person, a contact analogous to that established in Palestine between Jesus and those who followed him. It means above all to follow Christ on his existential way, to commit oneself with all the strength of personal, enlightened liberty to union with Christ—a union ontologically concluded by him and endowed with the strength of his Spirit, enabling man to live the same style of life and leading him to a common destiny of eternal encounter with the Father who has called us from the very beginning. This way is the way of the Gospel in the whole of its dynamic structure. It is the way of the incarnation (openness to grace in the judgment and activity of each man), the way of the cross (fidelity in the struggle against sin), and the way of the resurrection (anticipation and preparation of the eschatological life).

This synthesis was elaborated, though in different forms of expression, by St. John and especially by St. Paul.

The Liturgy

There exist between liturgy and morality (taught and practiced) on the one hand essential links, and on the other hand an important distinction. Catechesis must take these links as well as the distinction into account. Both refer to the content and the forms of liturgy and morality.

Christian morality depends in its content on sacramental liturgy, in the sense that the practice of all the Christian virtues should be under the impulse of the grace conferred on us by the Lord in the sacraments. Inversely, all the sacraments are destined to make grace active, and this extends beyond the time of the actual liturgical celebration. The call to which God awaits my response can be formulated thus: Become more and more, through varied and strength-giving practice, what you are by the sacraments you receive. Even better, this should be expressed in the plural: All of you together become ...

Catechesis ought, therefore, to speak explicitly of these links. This subject can be developed along two paths, namely, the sacraments and the liturgical year. Beginning with the meaning of the sacraments, we should show what fundamental dispositions are necessary for receiving grace, and what general norms are necessary for rendering active the grace received. The sacraments are the basic structures of the Christian life. Their dynamic unity is found in the dialectic of the paschal mystery. Corresponding to these structures of the Christian life is the "spirituality of redemption," which we have described elsewhere.

But it is not possible to extract a complete morality in this way. A complete morality presupposes, in fact, an explicit and detailed anthropology, including the various ramifications of earthly values. The source of a Christian outlook on man at work, on

91

man in the family, and so forth, is not to be found in the liturgy, but in secular life christianized, because the Lord gives his grace at every moment and in every place, without being bound by a liturgical celebration.

The liturgical year offers a sheaf of aspects all belonging to the central paschal mystery. To bring catechetical elaboration directly into relationship with the liturgical year has, therefore, the double advantage of being based on "actual" liturgical elements and of preparing the faithful to participate with more enlightened dispositions in the celebration of the liturgical seasons. But here also it is only a question of certain aspects and not of a complete morality. If liturgical catechesis is particularly suited to putting all the faithful, irrespective of their age or background, into the moral and religious dispositions appropriate to the celebration of the paschal mystery, especially the Eucharist, it has the disadvantage of not being particularly adapted to needs or to individual and positive capacities—for example, at the time of adolescence, or within the family. For this reason, if it is sometimes lawful to choose "linking-up points" (soon to be put aside), it is better, as soon as the actual subject of the catechesis is broached, not to indulge arbitrarily in occasional, artificial, and meaningless applications, but to put frankly in evidence the real distinctions and real links at the heart of the Christian mystery.

Concerning the forms of expression, there exist between the liturgy and the present morality two aspects of unity. If morality in the broad sense means the total response of man to God, then the response which consists in expressing the theological virtues under a symbolic form in the liturgy is, to a certain degree, the principal one.

Then, because of the valid exchange made between the strict and broad sense of these terminologies, the moral form, which is not, strictly speaking, liturgical, can give expression to an act of worship, and vice versa. For example, the Old Testament, speaking of the worship of false gods, labels it as fornication; and St. Paul, speaking of chastity, puts the faithful on their guard against the profanation of their bodies, which are the temples of the Spirit. One would cause confusion, however, by trying to express all anthropology in terms of cult, or even by only making use of terms of cult to speak of the relationships between man and God. This provokes a foreshortening of one's range of vision, and prevents one from seeing man in his connatural diversity.

For this reason, without suppressing the aspects of unity which we have indicated, it seems to us that it is above all the distinction between the forms of the liturgy and the forms of morality which demands our attention. The liturgy is expressed in symbols, morality in acts and considered principles. The language of the liturgy is based on a choice of biblical extracts and symbolical gestures which are performed in the present. But the laws of this language are based on a double criterion: on the one hand, the existential link of the events of the history of salvation to which the liturgy looks back; and on the other, the interplay of symbols and their analogies. Hence there is an important consequence here for catechesis on revealed truth and Christian living. The content of the liturgy, such as it is expressed by symbolic forms, is the same as that of truth and practice; but the liturgical use of the interplay of symbols implies neither an exegesis of the biblical texts being used, nor conclusions concerning the structure of Christian living. In a word, we find ourselves faced with radically different categories of thought.

Corresponding to the different categories of thought are different categories of expression. The categories must not be mixed so as to cause confusion. A kind of language which gives suitable expression to the "Christian response" will be used, but each according to its own laws. The language of the liturgy is immediately suited to the symbolic actions of the sacraments. Morality is expressed in fact by actions (witness of Christian living) and in theory by forms of reflective thought, namely, doctrinal and sapiental forms.

Life Witness

Existential signs translated into life have an essential function in revelation and, therefore, in catechesis. Throughout the whole of the Old Testament, whenever God wants to reveal to the whole of his people how he would like to see them live, he inspires especially certain persons whom he puts in evidence to act in a particular way. This divine moral pedagogy is put into practice fully in the earthly life of Jesus, and it remains faithful to itself throughout the evolution of the Christian people. Figures to be put in evidence belong, therefore, to catechesis much more than do concrete examples which serve to illustrate abstract principles. Men, women, and children living as true Christians are witnesses to the response to God's call translated into life. These testimonies, even when they do not appear to be heroic, constitute an authentic and indispensable source of moral catechesis.

The catechetical value of testimony concerns, above all, awareness of the fact that Christian morality is basically a response to a call from God. The figures to be put in evidence are, therefore, especially those in whom this awareness of a call from God was the most conspicuous. Moreover, moral catechesis must be "interiorized" by penetrating into the intentions of the characters and stressing that the dynamism which animated them was a charity surpassing simple human strength, a charity which is the fruit of a gift of God, which the Holy Spirit communicates to the Christian people, by participation in the charity which animates Jesus himself.

By choosing these testimonies from the lives of Christian "heroes," one can apply a pedagogy which is particularly to be recommended for pre-adolescents. Pedagogy based on a process of identification (without confusion) is, moreover, valid for all ages and backgrounds, provided one takes sufficiently into account the differences in application which each case requires. Like the pedagogy of ideal, the pedagogy of hero needs to be conducted with great prudence. Otherwise, overly human tendencies to conceit and competition favor the illusions of visionaries and the self-sufficiency of voluntarists, all of which end in disillusioned and discouraged setbacks. True Christian testimonies, on the contrary, encourage humility and confidence.

Following upon what has just been said, catechesis on morality could be based on an event of the moment. However, we will take up this subject after we have discussed the questions relating to reflective thought.

Testimonies, whether they be heroic or ordinary, only have a limited catechetical value. We have already pointed out—in reference to the awareness of a call (especially communion through charity), the transcendent aspect of Christian conduct, and the invitation to generosity—that the catechetical value of testimonies is a privileged one; but it remains necessarily defective when faced with other exigencies, namely, the duty of catechesis to explain the Christian meaning of the different human tendencies and aspirations (for example, sexuality and world development), and to show with sufficient clarity at the appropriate age the objective structures of moral conduct (for example, the different forms or degrees of obligation and their consequences).

Reflection and Formulation

It is important to recognize that diversity in ways of thinking is normal and valid, and has a great influence on the spirit of catechesis on morality and on the arrangement of the instruction.

95

One should have reasonably clear ideas, in this connection, on three points.

1. The first point concerns the different ways of thinking arising from the three dimensions of the moral order. Catechesis on morality must first of all emphasize the objective order willed by God. This way of thinking is based on laws which command respect for certain values considered in themselves (in God's keeping). The instruction takes the form of "commandments" more or less (and often with notable "interpolations") linked up with the Decalogue of the Bible. One could also take the virtues as dispositions necessary to the keeping of the commandments, perhaps by comparing two series, for example the cardinal virtues and the last seven commandments—obedience and the fourth commandment, as a more specific instance.

Catechesis on morality must also emphasize the free subjectivity willed by God. This way of thinking is particularly bound up with the dynamism by which man tends to his own perfection. This tendency and the result it is destined to achieve are also willed by God. But this dynamism functions within the field of values. Man finds himself in the presence of "facts"—the world, himself, other people—on which he makes a value judgment, that is to say, he becomes aware of the connection between these facts and the progress of his own perfection. Hence morality is expressed in terms of a value to be accomplished. Instruction is arranged according to a hierarchy and cohesion of values, for example (exterior) values of conditioning, (interior) values of vitality, (social and communal) values of comprehension and communion. In this way of thinking, the virtues, considered as forces of development, belong to values of superior vitality.

To the two ways of thinking which we have just mentioned, there correspond two kinds of formulas. The objective order and the commandments which distinguish it are best expressed in doctrinal principles of morality; a judgment which results from an awareness of the relationship between the facts of existence and man's perfection or happiness, and the sense of values therein included, is best expressed in sapiential principles.

Third and lastly, there must be an emphasis on man's interpersonal relationships with God. The development of this way of thinking is generally to be found in treatises on spirituality.

2. Our second point concerns the complementary ways of thinking arising from two perspectives of the moral question.

Analytical and static thought defines each action according to its nature and its accomplishment in conformity with this nature. All actions are seen to form part of an established order. It is also considered possible to go on classifying each action according to this order. This is done especially by authoritative declarations. Moreover, moral judgment finds its surest support in official declarations. It is obvious, however, that there are urgent needs which do not accord or even fit in at all with the prescriptions of the established order.

On the other hand, synthetic and dynamic thought sees the natural law and man's life as a whole, existing together in harmony in a material world which man must continue to transform. God, in fact, has entrusted man with real liberty so that he may bring a certain initiative into his use of it. The order established by God is creation in evolution. This includes the task entrusted to man to work at establishing an order, for any order corresponding to a particular moment of evolution becomes disorder if it prevents normal evolution, and a new situation calls for a new order. For this reason, it is impossible to determine fully the moral value of a particular action (except for a complete break with the living God or a direct attempt on a life which has a perfect right to develop), if one does not take into account the influence of this action in the total movement towards the final realization of a man's life viewed as a whole. It is not possible, furthermore, to codify morality in its entirety, and there is even great danger of abuse in the attempt at codification—or in the routine referral to codes. Likewise, declarations of the voice of authority should never be used in such a way that they will suppress the moral sense of the Christian, who receives light from the Spirit—never be used, that is to say, as if they will show in detail how he is personally to follow his route towards the final end. Moreover, in new situations, a certain accord of moral judgment among the sincere faithful often anticipates the official declarations. However, such a moral consensus is only valuable if it is elaborated on in its dynamic perspective, if it is taken to the interior of the "established limits" by way of the fundamental truths of creation and Christian redemption.

3. The third and last main point which we must keep in mind in preparing and presenting our catechesis on morality is that it is necessary to refer to norms and the circumstantial situation when one makes a personal moral judgment. This is very important.

When norms and situation are separated, one falls into extremes which are false. A morality which is extreme in its principles ignores the fact that life cannot be classified in all its departments. An ethic which views the situation exclusively ignores the fact that what is unique in situations, has a connection with the basic facts of life. Individual conscience is the meeting place of norms and situation. The moral judgment must refer to an objective norm if it is to be valid. There is, however, a multiplicity of norms. A norm can be considered from the point of view of man's last end (all the rest being means or ways), from the point of view of a supreme value—the others occupying a prescribed place in the scale of values, or from the point of view of the gift of God received at baptism as an invitation, received through preaching as a dynamism, and developed by means of the other sacraments.

A norm also can be considered (that is, be the object of a reflection) according to different procedures (of reflection), namely, through an analytical consideration which concentrates on one or several means, or through a general consideration of objectives which acknowledges the total (human) significance of a voluntary act extending through several stages. This is why there is a difference between a judgment on the morality of obtaining money dishonestly to help a poor man and a judgment on the morality of a surgical transplantation which consists of a voluntary gift from one person to another.

A norm can be expressed in doctrinal or sapiential terms. It can also be adopted from the conduct or judgment of another person who inspires trust (the Christian's principal point of reference is the life of Jesus Christ). But conscience does not work automatically. One cannot apply as in mathematics a "rule of three." Each situation has something which is peculiar to it, and these "contingencies" also contain a call from God which must be recognized. And, following what was said earlier concerning a dynamic morality, all that is exterior to the individual will has an element of indetermination in relation to the free act. It is precisely the business of personal responsibility to remove this indetermination by free self-determination. A person can only act "in conscience" if he acts freely. Catechesis must, therefore, show the necessary "references" (authority, example, reason), but also train consciences to assume their own responsibility. Conscience need not fear that God will punish with unhappy consequences an involuntary error of judgment. On the contrary, trust in God will give it the necessary strength to respond to the light.

In all of the points which we have considered, we see that Christian morality is based on the primacy of charity. This is true even at the purely human level. It is more completely true at the Christian level which is founded in faith.

Christian charity, threefold, is: charity which is not simply an objective law, but above all a dynamism corresponding to the supreme value, because it is an interpersonal communion; a dynamic charity which goes on increasing in height, depth, and

99

extent; and charity loyally attentive to God and necessarily inventive with him, in Jesus Christ, and in the strength of the Spirit.

2. THE HUMAN BACKGROUND

The study of man-in-a-situation includes in the first place some reflection on philosophical and religious anthropology. But anthropology takes on various forms according to psychological development and sociological influences.

Psychology

The presentation of morals and the formation of consciences must be mindful of the possibilities offered by the development of the moral judgment. Several primitive norms of behavior exist: automatism—the need of repeating some determined actions following a fixed scheme; instinct; repressed tendencies; custom; formalism—which does not always take circumstance into account.

In passing from infantile psychology to the adult attitude, man must conquer or integrate these influences, according to whether they are favorable or unfavorable to the personal engagement. This one is truly Christian when it is the answer to the call which God has addressed to us through Christ.

Sociology

The moral conception will certainly present some nuances which are related to the particular milieu of the family, of the social class, of the school, and so forth. The principal contemporary petitions, however, are more universal because they are more conditioned by the modern world in its whole.

3. COMMUNICATING THE MESSAGE

Preparation

There are various possibilities here in choosing a focal point for our presentation of morality. We can, for instance, choose the ten commandments, or the Christian virtues, or the example of Christ. At any rate, the elaboration of a schema must insert the essential truths which are the fundamental principles of other truths. Individual psychological evolutions, in addition, may suggest preferences for such and such a catechetical procedure which best corresponds to the psychological aptitudes of a various age group.

The education of a very young child is influence above all by the atmosphere of the educational milieu. It is important, then, that the child realize that the catechist himself loves and obeys God.

The child of nine to twelve years will admit without much difficulty that he must follow rules in all that he does, even in games. He is taught, therefore, to observe the commandments of God, which are the rules of life. In the beginning, the importance of rules for a child is that they are necessary conditions for obtaining a result which are interiorly controllable. Rules will help him progressively to discover the interior aspect of moral conduct.

Morality lived according to the virtues seems to be especially suitable for adolescents. They have become aware of certain values which they hold, though not in any overview way. Moreover, adolescents are disposed to imitate a person who incarnates these virtues in an admirable way. The bringing together of the values which they most esteem and the ideal of their own personality, in effect places them in front of their ideal. This is certainly a great help in their moral and religious education, but on the other hand it is important to avoid the danger of unrealism

101

and anthropocentrism. As far as concrete possibilities are concerned, the adolescent's ideal may not correspond to the true will of God. The excellence which he may aspire to may still remain on the plane of purely human effort. He should be helped, therefore, if this is the case, to ask himself whether he is in reality actually desirous of placing God and his grace in the service of his own human wants, rather than wishing to engage himself in the service of God, of making himself active in God's supernatural plan of salvation.

The important point in the formation of youth is the orientation that their profound affection takes—love of oneself, of others, of God.

Adults, finally, have special problems which must be resolved: those pertaining to conjugal morality, to work, to civic activity. Yet, what characterizes adult morality is not so much the adult's professional or civic specialization, as his entire active integration in the community. All his moral formation, therefore, must lead up to the realization of his becoming a "Christian adult," that is, one who knows that his life is a participation in the paschal life of Christ.

All Christian morality, therefore, must eventually be paschal, for the mystery of salvation is a paschal mystery. Paschal morality is that active attitude of the Christian which, in relying on the grace of God, and in doing the will of God, aspires to and also realizes full communion in charity with Christ.

Procedure

All catechesis is a dialogue in which God's word is spoken, but also sought, discovered, meditated on, penetrated, applied, and expressed.

This combination of presentation on the part of the catechist and the activity on the part of those instructed must draw freely on the various procedures corresponding to the content and forms of revelation.

For example, for young children moral training should be based on the existential signs of the Christian family. Moral catechesis for older children can be based on the Bible, and be linked up with the liturgy on an elementary level. For pre-adolescents, the pedagogy can be that based on a hero, for adolescents that based on values and their exegencies—exegencies now realized in a more personal manner. For older adolescents, moral catechesis ought to be based on the Gospel and be linked up with the liturgy at a higher level. For adults, the catechesis should be based on the axiological analysis of a situation in view of a synthesis of all the catechesis that has preceded. At all times, however, and for all age groups, the catechesis must have Jesus Christ as its central point of reference.

The chief element in a catechesis on morality which aims at awakening a personal response to God, consists, no doubt, in the effort to reëcho the call of God as manifested in the invitation given to us by Jesus, and in the response which Jesus himself gives to his Father. Let us avoid, then, dictating answers of a general nature. Let us not fail to give our students the necessary time for contemplating Christ, for giving him who hears God's word the chance to discover for himself that a response to God is demanded from God. Let us give him time enough to discover what that response of his is to be.

VI

Sin and Penance

1. GOD'S WORD

THE positive response which man makes to God is intricately bound up with its counterpart, namely, the refusal to respond— or rather, the response which consists in refusing to welcome God's call. It will be readily understood, therefore, that certain pitfalls must be avoided in the treatment of this subject: the danger of minimizing sin, by closing one's eyes to its universality and malice; of practically passing over it in silence, because it is not a pleasant subject; of unduly limiting its horizons, by speaking of it merely as a matter for confession; of unduly extending its domain, by giving the name "sin" to anything outside the theoretical exigencies of an ideal; or of losing sight of the incomplete development of the moral judgment and the relative lack of freedom in the performance of an action.

105

What is more, if there is one subject which may not be isolated from its living context, it is this. Sin is not a chapter in its own right; it is an element in each of the chapters of the mystery of salvation, which is the mystery of redemption. The subject could be introduced somewhat after the manner of the opening reel of a film: the living characters appear in a jumbled interplay of relationships which gives them unity. The film itself will reveal just what exactly these relationships are. So sin must be looked upon as a vast context, into which the following make their entry: man, tempted from without and from within, at grips with forces which seem to him stronger than his liberty; man, conscious of having freely yielded to sin; man, entering upon the way of repentance, penance, and conversion; God, thwarted in his loving designs by man's rebellion and ingratitude; God, ever mindful of the sinner; God, ready to forgive; God, fighting with man against the common enemy; Christ, at the heart of all this activity, who takes away the sins of the world; and the Church, community and institution both, in whom and for whom the Saviour carries out the deliverance of the world.

The Bible

In the Bible, sin is revealed in and through history. Each element of the subject of sin is, to a certain degree, in a state of continual development, but what emerges most clearly from the association between the different elements is the tension between the action of sinful man and the action of God who wills to save him.

We shall not insist here on such aspects as the growth of the moral sense or the sense of responsibility. We shall, however, try to give a brief description of what, according to the Bible, constitutes the reality of sin and the sinful state of humanity, and God's continual sovereignty and mercy.

The Bible gives us a kind of backlog of "example stories" which show sin as the refusal to depend (that is, even apart from the special bonds uniting the people to God). The chief of these examples is the account of man's origins. Placed by his very origin in a state of dependence on God, who is his happiness, man claims a moral autonomy, and, in his pride, rebels against God. Humanity finds itself in a state of sin. God gives proof of his mercy, however, by promising to give man the final victory over the forces of evil which assail him.

God's special gesture towards his people places them in a state of covenant, which means that God is recognized as the sovereign of his people, their assured protector, and their faithful spouse to whom fidelity is obliged. Sin is infidelity. It has four forms.

God wills that "his justice" (the order which he seeks to establish) be observed by his people, especially in their social relationships. But the proud self-sufficiency and egotism of the rich and powerful is bent on the oppression of the weak.

Pride and moral negligence lead to foolhardiness. By practicing a formalistic cult, the people imagine that they can count on God (present and worshiped in the Temple) to rescue them from the other nations, even though they do not observe his justice.

When God does not satisfy the desires of his people as well and as quickly as they would like, they turn their attention to other sources of security and happiness.

Finally, the most radical and fatal form of infidelity is the refusal to enter into the progressive dynamism of the covenant. For God's fidelity is a love desirous of giving itself more and more in depth and in extent. It is a call to advance in interiorization and to surpass oneself—for example, by having a sense of belonging to God which is produced more from the heart than from physical descent, as seen in the ritual sign; or by welcoming non-Iraelites into the nation which enfolds all those of upright heart. Every new stage of union with God increases man's moral and religious obligations. But man is unfaithful to this call to advance and turns in on himself; he is wary of these increasing obligations; he defends himself by a rigid conformity to the past, to nationalism and legalism; he abandons himself to moral and religious sclerosis, which is opposed to the life God wishes to give and to make grow.

The cause of these sins of infidelity is always in some way or other presumptuous pride and weak mistrust: man wants to lean on no one but himself, and he lacks sufficient trust in God's help. He is shut up within himself, and he seeks elsewhere than in God the guarantee of his happiness. Faithlessly, he abandons God.

Yet even when he abandons God, even when he refuses to give himself, the man of the Bible knows that his destiny is in God's hands. He knows that the sinner depends on God's "judgment," a judgment which God does not fail to execute. But God recalls through his prophets what this judgment means. Yahweh does not will to abandon man to the consequences of his sin and to punish him with death. On the contrary, he wishes man to be converted so as to receive God's pardon and live. If God sends chastisement, its primary purpose is a healing conversion; it is only if man hardens himself in his will to sin that he incurs that final chastisement which plunges him into irremediable death. But from the moment when he is ready to be converted, man can count on God's mercy for his purification and salvation.

These tensions existing between God's invitation to a more perfect covenant and sin, and the threat of eternal punishment and the mercy shown to those who are not hardened to evil, all are to be found throughout Jesus' public life, and they reach their peak moment in the "hour" of the redeeming Christ. The coming of the kingdom of God is also the coming of "divine judgment," a judgment which, in many respects, is primarily merciful. God invites man to a more perfect love and conversion and entrusts the first stage in the execution of judgment to his Messiah in two ways: Christ pardons the sins of those who repent, and he threatens the obstinate with perdition so that all at least may avoid final impenitence.

The redeemer sent in God's behalf is involved to the utmost

limits in the struggle against sin. He submits to being assailed by the most violent of man's sinful passions against the Messiah. Jesus remains faithful unto death to his Father and to the love for men which he has come to show in his Father's name. Thus he becomes the means of purification given by God to humanity. Thus God institutes through his Messiah and in his Church a power of merciful "judgment" which confers his forgiveness and restores true life, a life which takes up once more its growth towards the full realization of the new and eternal covenant.

The Liturgy

The real links existing between the liturgy and sin are, therefore, more numerous than those uniting the sacrament of penance and sin. The whole of Christian liturgy has necessarily an element of "conversion" and of efficacy relating it to the triumphant deliverance from sin.

Baptism is the uprooting of sin; confirmation gives us the strength to bear witness against the "world," in its pejorative sense, and in the world, in the usual sense; the Eucharist, above all, is the sacramental sacrifice of continual purification, for it is a meal for sinners, fortifying them for the long journey and for combat in their march to heaven.

All the other sacraments have a similar dimension of conversion, but of these the sacrament of penance is directly aimed at the remission of personal faults committed after baptism. The liturgical renewal invites us to rediscover the wealth of meaning inherent in certain aspects of the "celebration" of this sacrament which, for a long time now, has remained blurred, especially the community aspect of our reconciliation into the Church.

One could likewise say that all the liturgical seasons contain an aspect of struggle against sin, but that Lent merits special attention as a time of penance and preparation for conversion, as a paschal rebirth.

109

Life Witness

The existential signs belonging to the history of the Church, especially current history, ought, like the Bible and the liturgy, to make us more aware of two elements: the reality of sin and the reality of the fight against sin. These same signs ought likewise to make us dig deeper at two levels: the level of personal responsibility and the level of participation in the responsibility of the whole Church. At this stage, three aspects should be put in relief.

There is first of all sin in the personal life of each one of us, sincerity in recognizing it, the will to repent, and living testimony to the strength which the sorrowing sinner draws from God's mercy. The finest testimonies in this respect are those borne by the saints. Literature may also provide an illustration of personal experience.

Secondly, there is sin in the Church and the need for continual reform at the community level, with everyone sharing in this twofold responsibility.

Sin in this instance does not mean primarily faults arranged according to species, sins which can be recognized by every Christian in his examination of conscience. Sin in the Church is the continuation of the public life we have already come across in the Old Testament and the Gospel; it is the hedging, faithless response of the entire people to the manifestation and accomplishment of God's kingdom. The effects of this guilty negligence are to be seen, above all, in the Church as the "sign" of Jesus Christ. She ought to be the universal "testimony" par excellence of charity and the other evangelical virtues, and yet certain of her ordinary (or rather, routine) aspects make it a "scandal" for the members of her household, as well as for those outside.

This conciliar era which we are living in reminds us of our common guilt and the urgency of a common reform in which each must take his part.

The awakening of the community conscience and the energy with which the reform has been undertaken are both the signs and the fruits of the action of the Holy Spirit in the Church at grips with sin.

The third and last aspect is sin throughout the world, and the duty imposed on us of defending ourselves against contagion and of helping others, by God's grace, to break away from their sinful state.

This double duty is not mutually exclusive, as if one could not help others while, at the same time, defending oneself; the two aspects are complementary and even "rub shoulders." By "watching and praying" we become much more aware of the needs of others; by helping others we become more cautious lest we ourselves should be swept adrift, as we take care to become more and more imbued with the leaven of grace which must help us transform the world in Christ. This struggle obviously requires the active presence of Christians in the world at large and in each of its divisions. Let us not forget, however, that the laws of the struggle are completely different from those obeyed by the world. The laws peculiar to the struggle for the kingdom of God give contemplative prayer leading to intercession a real value, while noisy protests are often less effective than the discreet testimony of charity inviting its recipient to draw closer to God. Our testimony joins that of Jesus especially at this point.

Reflection and Formulation

Taking its rise from living sources, reflective thought develops into doctrine and wisdom; and the decision to concentrate on one element or other leads in theory and in practice to different kinds of spirituality. A particular thought or a particular attitude is "dynamic" if it is primarily based on relationships which, in their turn, are modified by progression or retrogression. Let us examine three kinds of relationships.

111

There is, first, the relationship between sin and the deliverance from sin. The true significance of sin and the dispositions befitting the sinner can only be understood in the light of their relationship with what preceded the sin (namely, the path of deliverance from sin). The sense of sin, therefore, contains three inseparable elements: a horror of evil, the need of salvation which man is incapable of obtaining for himself, and trust in the Lord who saves all who do not harden themselves in sin. A comparison between what precedes sin and what follows it suggests that certain customary expressions should be modified to give a more dynamic perspective. It is not merely a question of regaining a lost innocence, of turning back to a state preceding sin; it is, above all, a "return forward"; the sin itself is a turning backward, and "conversion" is to take up once more the march forward. The God who calls us is always in front of us, and penance is a form of spiritual progress.

Secondly, there are the relationships between persons involved in the history of sin and of deliverance. Just as sin should not be isolated, so the sinner should not be left to himself. Psychologically speaking, this isolation of the sinner is inadvisable, but, above all, it is false from an ontological point of view. It is important, therefore, to show, in relation to the three elements of the sense of sin, the part played in the drama by the person who misuses his liberty and other human beings, both actively and passively; by God and him whom God has sent as our redeemer in the fight against sin; and by the Church as an institution which has received from Christ the power to forgive, but also as a community which is existentially engaged in the struggle against sin.

Perspectives such as these indicate a real possibility of living "penance" as an "encounter." Experience proves that for many persons, for children and young people as well as for adults, God's mercy as shown to them personally was the occasion of privileged moments of encounter.

Last of all, there is the relationship between penance as a virtue and penance as a sacrament.

There must be unity in the collaboration of sacramental grace with the active dispositions of the penitent. The first is by no means the effect of the second. On the contrary, grace comes to the help of human weakness. The grace of the sacrament transforms the sinner in all that concerns his "return forward" to God: repentance, firm purpose, constant humility and sincerity, energy in resisting recurrent temptations. In certain cases, the need for an adequate conversion and reconciliation makes the reception of the sacraments obligatory, both from the ontological-theological point of view and the ecclesial point of view. Moreover, the sacrament requires the sinner to do all in his power to make himself receptive to God's healing and transforming action, and this by the way of preparation as much as by way of subsequent cooperation.

It is also essential to distinguish between the different levels of human anthropology and Christian existence present within the unity between virtue and sacrament. Repentance is not to be confused with remorse; a conversion producing a strong emotional reaction may not be at all strong at the moral level; the direct effect of the sacrament is to be found at the theological level (in direct contact between God and man).

Reconciliation is not necessarily experienced emotionally, any more than one can be sure from the psychical point of view that one will not repeat the sins he has confessed. If grace also helps us to change our habits, this moral effect is only produced by applying our liberty according to the usual norms of application—for example, in patience.

Though there is, as we have said above, an essential unity between penance considered as virtue and penance considered as sacrament, we must also be aware of the various shifts of emphasis on this unity. The history of the Church unfolds before our eyes the changes in awareness of each succeeding epoch, of dif-

113

ferent temperaments, and of the religious attitudes proper to the different stages of the life of an individual. If, therefore, a spirituality of penance ought to be sacramental and moral as well (or ascetical and existential), it may nevertheless be opportune to emphasize one aspect rather than another. These emphases may be compared to the relationship between the four requirements of the sacrament: contrition, confession, absolution, and satisfaction. As practices and spiritualities have evolved, each of these requirements has been stressed in turn. We shall briefly indicate three cases:

1. It is possible to stress the psychological and psychic advantages of penance. In this case, attention is drawn to the avowal which liberates, or to penance as a compensation which restores balance. But it would be wrong to give more importance to these aspects than to the ontological ones. The effect of every sacrament has, above all, the theological plane as its objective.

2. When the stress is given to the sacramental power of the Church as evidence of the Lord's merciful judgment, the four requirements are presented as follows. The sinner must be willing to admit that he deserves punishment (satisfaction). It is imposed on him by the Church in the Lord's name, and the Church communicates to him the divine pardon (absolution). At present, the chief practice of penance imposed by the Church is the avowal of faults (confession). The avowal also enables the priest to act as a judge, but he is not asked to assure an exact balance between the degree of guilt and the punishment. Basically, it is only God who can judge with equity. It is the penitent's duty, above all, to confess that he admits his sin, that he repents (contrition), and that he begs for pardon, while putting his trust in the Lord.

3. Another aspect of the emphasis given to penance as a sacrament and the role of the Church is the ecclesial, community one. The sacramental is inserted into a "liturgical celebration" constructed on lines similar to those of other liturgical ceremonies. The advantages of such an emphasis are numerous and counter-

act minimalizations which had taken root. Confession is no longer considered a purely personal matter, a disagreeable necessity, a formality to be finished with as quickly as possible. It is once more understood as a prayer of the whole Church made in common for each other's benefit, a regular enacting of a Christian attitude in a fitting emotional environment to which sufficient time is devoted for it to be carried out with care. However, as always happens, a particular emphasis (even when it consists of "common" celebrations) runs the risk of neglecting other important elements. It must not happen that the sacrament of penance should seem to be nothing more than a prolonged and solemn recitation of a *"confiteor"* in common, thereby robbing the sense of one's personal sins of its keenness.

In other words, sacramental and existential aspects and personal and community attitudes must always complete each other. Existential and personal problems, moreover, are the province of several pastoral activities: catechesis, the administration of the sacrament of penance, spiritual direction and pastoral dialogue.

Following the dynamic presentation of relationships, catechesis should also show how the sacraments of penance and the Eucharist draw upon and complete each other.

2. THE HUMAN BACKGROUND

Man's psychological attitude towards sin and penance depends to a great extent on the way the "disorderly action" is understood and the reparation it may exact. There are three levels of attitude: the legal, the moral, and the religious. The person who places himself only on the legal plane knows that even an involuntary breach of the regulations exposes him to a penalty. If he finds a way to escape, he will congratulate himself. On the moral plane, the voluntary fault introduces an interior disorder in the person. Eventually, he allows this disorder to be transformed into a disorderly inclination which progressively gains in strength. The person must therefore react by mortifying himself. Sin, which offends God and is a breach of friendship with him, is a disorderly action seen in its religious light. The reparation will first of all be the work of God, who wants to reëstablish this friendship, to reconcile the sinner (2 Cor. 5, 19).

The "disorderly action" takes on a special nuance in each of these planes if it harms other men, and reparation of the defect thus becomes a necessity.

Psychology

The psychological evolution of a person who commits the breach and who makes reparation, follows, on the whole, the same pattern which the development of the community and which other personal values have given to the fault.

A child sees his faults in a concrete way, in relation to the various persons whom he frequents, and in relation to the consequent action which someone may give him to carry out. He will judge his faults above all according to the visible result of his faults. Even so, his first regret may consist at first in the wish not to be punished. Too, there is the possibility that he has learned that it is noble to ask forgiveness from someone whom he has hurt.

The school-age child learns to make more objective judgments, to see in what degree of disproportion from the standard order his disorderly conduct is. He will, by way of establishing a compensatory rule, admit to the validity of imposed punishments for the breaking of rules, and that the punishment is applicable to all. But he will pay less attention to the breach in a personal relationship which his conduct has caused. Therefore, in our catechesis on the action of God and the part of Christ in the sacrament of penance, we must attempt to correct whatever is unilateral in this attitude of the child.

In early adolescence, the personal moral aspect of the disorderly action comes to the forefront of conscience. The conscience has been disturbed by an experience which the adolescent does not feel in full control of. In later adolesence a refinement takes place regarding the meaning of personal relationships, which leads to a greater comprehension of the reality of the community. Consequently, the later adolescent comes to a better understanding of the true essence of sin, and is also better enabled to make reparation in its personal and ecclesial dimensions.

The adult, finally, must synthesize within himself his attitudes on sin and penance on all three levels—objective, subjective, and interpersonal, for man's relationship to God comprises also the execution of his will regarding the moral order in man, and even in the practice of external laws which competent authority has lawfully promulgated.

There are, in the masculine and feminine temperaments both, weak and strong points as regards the practice of penance. If a boy is very rude in his mistakes, he is the more sincere in his objective avowal of these mistakes. The young girl is more easily inclined to confidences, but she meets difficulty in the fact that her confessor is a man—that is, she may think that because he is a man he will not be able to understand her. On the other hand, it is possible that a young girl will find it interesting to make herself heard by a man. In our catechesis, on this point we should state precisely that the penitent addresses himself above all to a confidant not merely of the human level, but to a man who represents Jesus Christ.

Sociology

The difficulties which what we might call the modern mind-set presents for the sacrament of penance, may be summed up as two erroneous tendencies: to have a morality without sin, and a religion without the Church. But even these tendencies are indica-

117

tive of an appeal by contemporary man to a concept and to a practice of authentic Christian penance.

Morality without sin denies the existence of God. It considers the sense of culpability to be unhealthy. Liberty it thinks of as an illusion. There is no evil so long as one does not commit notable injustice towards one's neighbors.

Religion without the Church regards sin to be an interior reality, strictly an individual thing—that is, for those who believe in God. Confession is seen as an outgrowth of clericalism.

In a revaluation of the authentic penance, one must come to know the meaning of the personal act that sin is, in its relation to God and to the community. One must come to a better vision of life, a better understanding of sin and reparation in the divine plan of salvation. Christ is the center of salvation, and he extends himself in the Church. The sacrament of penance must be viewed as directing one towards the holy Eucharist.

3. COMMUNICATING THE MESSAGE

The catechesis of the sacrament of penance cannot be concentrated on matters relating to the manner of confessing. It must be inserted, rather, in an education in the virtue of penance, and in an initiation to the sacrament seen in connection with the mystery of redemption, and above all in connection with the holy Eucharist.

Preparation

One must teach little children to ask forgiveness with the wish of becoming well behaved; the forgiveness by parents is the image, though imperfect, which we should foster of the forgiveness of God. Penitential catechesis will be framed, then, in the development of the meaning of responsibility, especially as it concerns the assumption of the consequences of one's acts.

Adolescents, therefore, must come to learn that they must have confidence in the mercy of God, yet also that patient effort is necessary in the struggle to correct one's defects.

The sacrament of penance is above all a gift of God, a paschal gift of Christ; it helps us enter into contact with the force of God, which is much more powerful in helping us to recover the state of grace, than are our weak human efforts, situated as they are alongside our disordinate inclinations. On the other hand, the sacrament of penance is not in the first place a means of moral progress—it is not destined, that is to say, to place God in the service of our personal perfection. All the Christian religion, and therefore also the sacrament of penance, is a gift of God on the supernatural plane, and an answer of man through Christ. Grace penetrates our behavior only in a progressive way, and so we must preserve it with patience in our fight against our defects.

Procedure

In our catechesis, therefore, the examination of conscience will have its organic place, but it will also have a place sufficiently discreet in the entire penitential attitude. Its contents, the way in which it is formulated, and the use which is made of it, cannot be such that they make a man face himself in a negative and "minimalist" way. The examination of conscience should be so positive, rather, that it penetrates to those dispositions where our faults find nourishment. The examination of conscience must help us to revive our confidence in God and our desire to answer more generously to the grace of Jesus Christ.

It is convenient in our catechesis, moreover, to put in full light the most beautiful motives of contrition, those particularly which are attached to the love of Christ and to the fecundity of his grace in all his mystical body.

Let us remember that "confession" must not be limited to an enumeration of faults, but that it must be a profession of con-

119

trition. "I confess that I am a sinner, asking forgiveness of God and believing with confidence that God wants me to be reconciled with him, and that he wants to help me in my struggle to overcome my defects, through Christ, in his Church."

In this way, the relationship between absolution and the avowal of sins will become clearer to the catechized. In our catechesis, then, the satisfaction will not be presented as a kind of unimportant auxiliary. Satisfaction is a part of sacramental penance which helps the Christian in his faithful struggle to fight sin.

All catechesis on penance is planned so as to give the catechized an understanding of the true position of virtue and the sacrament of penance in the Christian life. Penance is not a wearisome formality reduced to its simplest form of expression, but, for the Christian aware of his "situation" as a sinner, it is a special gift of God to be used as fruitfully as possible. Faced with the more or less hidden temptation to sink into mediocrity by not reacting against habitual faults, we are armed now for the struggle and spiritual advancement by the sacrament of penance. When experience teaches us that our lives hardly correspond to the ideal that we have set for ourselves, and when we are dogged by a feeling of secret displeasure towards God, the sacrament of penance helps us to conform our will entirely to God's will, and to advance joyfully towards the goal which he has assigned to us.

The sacrament of penance above all enables us to participate more perfectly in the Eucharist, which is the center of our Christian life.

VII

Faith

IN its general sense and within the Christian mystery of salvation, faith signifies the entire Christian way of thought and life. Living in faith, then, becomes synonymous with living in Christ, or living according to the Spirit, or living on a supernatural plane. This total attitude implies knowledge and whole-hearted commitment, both leading through a conversion (always indispensable) to a communion (which is forever developing).

If the three theological virtues form part of faith in its general sense, there is one which we name "faith" in a particular sense in order to signify the element of knowledge contained within the Christian mystery. We must point out straightway that in this particular sense, too, faith implies a conversion (of mind) and a communion (of thought). Moreover, it will shortly become clear that we are dealing with a type of knowledge which presupposes a special kind of life in communion.

1. GOD'S WORD

The Bible

In the Bible, one of the most important attributes of God is contained in the words "He who knows." Not only does nothing remain hidden from him, but his knowledge is active; it commits God to a choice and an alliance (see Hos. 13, 5).

But God calls upon us to share his knowledge, that is to say, first of all to "know" him in his actions ("Now I know . . ."— Ex. 18, 11; Ps. 19, 7; 40, 12; 55, 10; 118, 75); then to know his ways of judging, his projects; and finally to communicate with him in interpersonal knowledge. This is achieved above all by Jesus Christ and in him.

Jesus is precisely he who lives with the Father in a shared knowledge which is unique (Mt. 11, 27), but he makes use of this privilege by imparting it to us (*ibid.*). Moreover, Jesus knows us, as he knows his Father (Jn. 10, 14–15), and in order that we may be capable of participating in his knowing activity, Jesus sends to us the Holy Spirit.

As the Acts of the Apostles makes clear, the Church is primarily the community of believers. In her, each one of us is called upon to increase in faith as an interpersonal knowledge of God, a knowledge still veiled here below, but which will be transformed in the beatific vision (1 Cor. 13, 13). In view of this end of our knowledge, we must seek to avoid the willful blindness of wrongdoers (Is. 1, 3; Jn. 1, 10; 17, 25), and obey the commandments in charity (1 Jn. 2, 3; 4, 7–8). For this complete receptiveness to God's gift will lead us to a knowledge of him in experience (Jn. 3, 16; 4, 16; 6, 70; 17, 3).

The Liturgy

The gift of faith, as an inner faculty, is given to us by the sacramental ministry of the Church, in communion with the faith

122

of the entire ecclesial community. This faith is expressed in prayer, especially in the liturgy, by words, by attitudes, and by gestures.

Life Witness

This gift should equally be expressed in the existential signs of everyday life, namely, in the consistency with which we put our Christian convictions into practice, in the words which give proof to our Christian mentality, and especially in our value judgments concerning events which call into question the very meaning of life.

An ecclesial environment where faith can be meditated on and expressed in the most fitting manner is by and large requisite for the development of faith in the members of the community, and for the spreading of that faith as a summons to those who have not yet heard the word of God, or whose knowledge of it is only slight.

Reflection and Formulation

It is necessary to reflect on the act of faith, and indeed, reflection is one of its dynamic elements. In our catechesis, since this act is specified by its object, it will undoubtedly become necessary to call attention to the essential contents of faith, but this should be done in connection with presenting the nature of the act of faith. In other words, knowledge of the faith—its contents—is important here only insofar as it is a necessary condition for discovering the knowledge of faith—that is, the personal nature of this knowledge.

Let us now go on to discuss the characteristics of the act of faith, that is, faith considered as the activity by which we know God in the signs of his revelation.

The object of faith (its content) is God himself, especially as

123

the author of our salvation. This salvation is realized in Jesus Christ by a gift of the Holy Spirit to the Church.

The mode or form of faith is the reading of the signs of revelation. It is a mode which is more intuitive than discursive, which is to say, it is a contemplation in the "mediation" of signs. The central sign is Jesus Christ constantly actual in the Church.

The supernatural faculty of faith is a gift of the Holy Spirit. This gift is not an inert thing received once and for all, but a continuous action whose effects are conditioned by our personal collaboration.

The dynamism and progress of faith consists in an interpersonal knowledge which binds our communal relationship with God, and which is endowed with a dynamic developmental force. Only, because of man's sinful nature, this dynamism is initially a demand for conversion—but this conversion, too, continues to develop.

The "movement" of our act of faith, once our free assent collaborates with the gift of the Spirit, begins with the reading of the signs, and this in turn leads us to recognize with sincerity that God speaks to us, and that his words are addressed to us. We must then learn to rely with trust and loyalty on him, so that we may know that the truth is ours, and that we may have the strength to act according to this truth. We must, finally, determine to live generously in communion of thought with God, and advance upon the path of total communion.

The result of faith, of course, is manifold. We are speaking here of active, developing result—the encounter with God in his word. We come, then, to know God as a person in his personal signs. We come to see God in Jesus, and actively to participate in his knowledge. We come to participate in the experience of the knowledge of faith communicated to the entire Church. We come to see mankind and the world through the eyes of Christ, perceiving therein the call of the Father. Therefore, we come to desire to radiate charity. We come to live with the Father in the light which radiates from Christ, *Lumen vitae.*

Let us now go on to make a comparison between the sapiential analysis of faith which we have just given, and the doctrinal explanation of a notional definition of faith which is now fairly current, namely, that to believe means to accept a truth on the testimony of another (this is supplied by the Church) without seeing (or understanding) for oneself.

The definition begins with the phrase "testimony of another"— but God who gives us his pledge is not simply another, apart from ourselves; he is not a stranger. Rather, he works within us, through his Spirit.

It says "without seeing"—but we must remember that faith sees in a light which, though veiled, is yet more perfect than natural light.

This faith, then, depends on knowledge received from the Church—but it leads to a personal conviction and to living participation.

This is a doctrinal truth—but it reaches, through doctrinal formulations, to the living God who reveals himself in Jesus Christ.

* * *

Having discussed the characteristics of faith, let us now go on to an analysis of the three dimensions of faith, which are the objective, the subjective, and the interpersonal.

Faith, which is knowledge of God in his word, occupies the same three dimensions as this word. When God speaks, he brings us to know facts and truths objectively. He appeals to our freedom, to our subjectivity, for he proposes that we should live according to a scale of values which requires a conversion in us. And by his word, he already makes binding a relationship which is an interpersonal and intersubjective reality.

Knowledge of faith is objective; the believer accepts objective facts and truths which are valid for all men at all times. However, we must avoid confusing objectivity and knowledge without personal commitment, for we are called upon to become involved in this objective reality. Therefore, these same truths have an axiological aspect: they are values. Revelation, which is truth *per se,* is true for me, and in two ways. First, it requires me to recognize its objectivity freely; and secondly, it is concerned with values, for what is true is that my welfare and my happiness reside in the supernatural goal which God reveals to me. But this supernatural end consists in perfect union with God, and this union begins precisely in the dialogue between God who reveals himself and man who recognizes him in faith. The fact that the activity of faith is developed in dialogue constitutes its intersubjective character.

These three dimensions allow us to understand more clearly the role played by faith in Christian life, for they belong to the whole of theologal life. On the one hand, we may stress the distinctions which exist between the three theological virtures, and we will then be obliged to relate the objective aspect to faith particularly, the subjective aspect to hope, and the intersubjective aspect to charity. On the other hand, it is important for us to underline that the intrinsic and constitutive relationships which exist between the virtue of faith and the virtues of hope and charity are particularly apparent in faith's subjective and interpersonal aspects. All of this can be expressed as follows. Theologal life consists in union with God. The act of faith fills the role of knowledge, by admitting the facts on which this union is founded and the truths which make their meaning explicit (this is objectivity); by accepting a free engagement of the will that this union with God constitutes the supreme value for us (subjectivity); and by becoming more and more aware of the relationships in which this union with God is lived (interpersonal).

This reality of the triple dimension occupied by faith is likewise to be found in the threefold form of trust which is one of its elements. There is, in fact, no conflict whatever between faith-trust and faith-knowledge. On the contrary, they complement one another. When we say that we believe firmly, we mean that we have a threefold trust: trust in "possessing" truth in certitude; trust in "being" oriented towards the supreme value, in security; and trust in "being with" God in faithfulness.

Let us recall at this point that the root of the Hebrew word used to designate faith means "solid support."

2. THE HUMAN BACKGROUND

Psychology

The three dimensions of faith are affected by the evolution of the psychological factors, and this is true not only from the point of view of intellectual progress, but also from the point of view of the different modes of trust.

The very young child has a total awareness and spontaneously trusts those around him with whom he lives in symbiosis. His faith becomes purified when he begins to make a distinction between forms of imagination and the present reality of the mystery which transcends his understanding.

The school-age child passes through a stage in which interest is largely directed towards objectivity, while trust, as yet unquestioning, is placed in the adults who teach him. His knowledge develops in an analytical way, and his memory is extremely retentive concerning the things he is taught. He advances in faith, seen as an encounter with the Lord, when he manages to pierce through the hard shell of rules which he must observe in order to acknowledge that he will be truly united to God if he obeys his will.

A real faith develops in the child in a conditioning of temporary credulity. We must avoid taking advantage of this kind of credulity, and encourage him to develop a personal faith.

A critical sense awakens in pre-adolescents, but it does not immediately result in psychological doubts, for they easily accept

127

as solutions answers to "difficulties" which are still of an objective nature.

However, with the adolescent, who is wrestling with his own personal problems, especially those of emotional disturbance, the case is quite different. Psychological doubt is born of his apprehension of the disharmony existing between the facts he is told to accept as a moral duty or as a divine revelation, and the imperfections of his freedom and the scale of values he is instinctively inclined to adopt.

This conflict is aggravated, moreover, by an ambiguous sociological situation: in the first place, the adolescent becomes aware that the official scale of values does not in fact serve as a practical criterion in the life of a great many Christians; and secondly, as he is very anxious to be "with" the times and even "with" future times, the adolescent is strongly attracted to new and non-Christian conceptions of life.

These trials have meaning in that they allow him to know, through faith and a purified view of faith, the real scope of his freedom which the Lord calls on him to exercise, the progressive support which he offers him, and the need for a conversion which opens the way to real communion.

Youth between the ages of eighteen and twenty-four stand on the threshold of adult life. Here faith undergoes a first synthesis which gives an intellectual and vital support to the personal conviction of the young believer. It as well makes him accept the responsibility of bearing witness within the community, and also of integrating all human values in his life as a Christian.

The adult, therefore, effects within himself and in relation to his temporal task, a solid union of objectivity and subjectivity in faith: He achieves the integration both in width and in depth. But the believing adult does not allow himself to be entirely monopolized by problems of temporal task or personal value, that is to say, by the horizontal structure of faith. It is principally in the direction of the vertical structure—the one which leads to an encounter with God in his living Word—that the "adult in faith" harmoniously fulfills every aspect (objective, subjective, interpersonal) of Christian "knowledge."

Sociology

The questions of faith which claim our attention from the sociological point of view are related first of all to exterior facts and verbal explanations which are specific for specific groups, and in the second place to the discovery of their causes insofar as they constitute sociological influences.

Facts. In dealing which each different group, the catechist should supply the answers to the following questions: What religious practices do these people observe? To what degree do these practices involve their conviction? What statements do they make on the subject of their faith? What beliefs do they profess? In the case of how many are these beliefs non-existent or doubtful?

Influences. Contemporary experience is one of an evolution which, on the one hand, gives rise to differentiations and consequently to a pluralism in modes of thought and life; and on the other hand, calls for the communal involvement of each individual.

The material and human wealth displayed in this evolution gives the secular temptation of "human sufficiency" a modern appearance. The mind of modern man, fascinated by the rapid progress of its positive sciences, is tempted to exclude other forms of knowledge. But faith requires man to acknowledge a truth surpassing scientific investigation and allows us to reach this truth through testimony which calls for our trust, and through symbolical forms which convey more by suggestion than what they express in the material sense.

The same may be said concerning the appreciation of action (from the axiological point of view). The two tendencies of the

E

modern mind are, on the one hand, its recourse to technology for temporal efficiency, with its social dimension—the organizing of mutual aid; and on the other hand, its desire for freedom, with its corresponding social dimension—the communion of people. But faith does not bring immediate solutions to technical problems, and on the individual as well as on the social plane it requires man to acknowledge that his freedom is not absolute.

The consequences of this generally accepted attitude are particularly obvious in the "humanist" field which is concerned with the appreciation of virtues. Modern virtues are attitudes of self-affirmation as characteristic expressions: lucidity and sincerity in action, courage and commitment to a task, clearly illustrate. True faith is not involved here, but rather a few of its distortions, which, unfortunately, are encountered fairly frequently in immature Christians whose faith comes into conflict with humanism. This humanism is being taken to task for engendering timid creatures who seek illusory consolations, and inefficient creatures who shirk the issue concerning human values. The direction we have been taking is a negative one which leads to the devaluation of faith, but it is equally possible to follow a positive course which leads to the purifying and revaluation of faith.

Starting from the same facts of contemporary experience (evolution, differentiation, pluralism, communal involvement), catechists will have to point out the weaknesses inherent in the human self-sufficiency we have just described, as well as the false interpretations on which the objections leveled against the Christian conception of life were founded. We must then develop the idea of the positive contribution which faith brings to modern aspirations (painstaking search for efficiency, mutual aid, freedom, communion). Faith requires that the self-sufficiency and exclusiveness of these aspirations should undergo a conversion, yet causes all their valid factors to be transcended, already in this life and especially in the eschatological completion which will be God's supreme gift to all men in Jesus Christ. It is precisely in this carefully reëxamined direction that a revival in the Church, which is thinking over her faith, is clearly beginning to emerge.

Thus we find ourselves once again faced with the ambiguity of all sociological situations. Even the revival in the Church is a source of disturbance for Christians who are too rigid in their understanding, while, on the other hand, the real difficulties which spring from the modification of social structures and mentalities are prompting leaders of the faith to create pastoral organizations which are better suited to cope with problems concerning faith, and to give a revitalized form of instruction on the faith.

Sociological contact between the different faiths in a pluralistic world presents an analogous problem. The ambiguity of this contact is demonstrated by the fact that it leads some to an attitude of indifference—all religions are equally valid; whereas it allows others to reach a firmer mutual understanding and to purify their conception of Christian revelation.

3. COMMUNICATING THE MESSAGE

The whole of catechetics must be a constant striving to give birth to an increasing faith.

Preparation

Catechesis on the theme of faith must also take into account the objections to faith which arise from psychological or sociological difficulties. It can be objected, for instance, that God is a medicinal invention of men which will help calm their fears and appease their desires; that the historical Jesus has been transformed by men into the Christ of faith, and endowed with imaginary attributes; that the Western Church is a parasite, since Christians are no better, socially or morally speaking, than non-Christians; that the Church, in countries apart from the Western

131

world, is an imported product to be rejected by those nations which have become conscious of their own identity and heritage. Needless to say, the catechetical replies to these objections must be based not only on the theme of faith, but also on all the other themes which we have discussed: the Church, the brotherhood of men, eschatological fulfillment.

Moreover, it would be advisable, when we *begin* our catechesis on the special theme of faith, to be explicit about the knowledge of faith, though perhaps in a general way. The subject of creation, for instance, will often require us to be precise about the different types of knowledge, for we will have to deal with positive science, the understanding of people's need of one another, faith in God.

Procedure

If catechesis rightly stresses in our day the proclamation of the word of God, and if it avoids a too lengthy examination of questions directly related to apologetics, this does not in any way mean that it intends to neglect the dogmatic foundations of the act of faith.

In the first place, all the points which we have made in our chapter on faith (and indeed, this is true of all the themes of catechesis) contain an important apologetic in both an implicit and an indirect way; and it will be the catechist's task to provide this apologetic *as the need arises*. In a sense, this kind of apologetics anticipates objections.

There is, however, a more systematic form of apologetics. In pre-catechesis, this kind of apologetics seeks to establish the preliminary conditions of the act of faith, not only regarding the contents of the message (the apologetic of pre-conversion), but also with regard to its form of presentation (whether symbolical, sapiential, or doctrinal). Next, it posits and elaborates on the reflective element in the act of faith, for even a man who is already a believer seeks to recognize explicitly the foundations of his faith and his reasons for believing.

In its third phase, this type of systematic apologetics must answer critical questions which arise in relation to beliefs which have been generally accepted by previous generations, but which create difficulties for the new generation. (This is, of course, a general way of expressing the matter; and we do not wish to suggest that other forms of individual difficulty will not arise and require solutions.) We do, in fact, live in a time which is examining anew both the philosophy of existence and the meaning of faith. This means, then, that our catechesis must allow for a double process of disintegration and reintegration. In dealing with young people, moreover, it is best that we not adopt a too rigid and unsympathetic attitude towards the objections; but on the other hand, we must also avoid giving free rein to a critical mind which presently is only capable of disintegrating material, and not of reintegrating it with new concepts. The most important and difficult task of our catechesis here is to help the catechized achieve a new and valid synthesis in his task of reintegration. Only when we ourselves have become sufficient masters in the art of helping others reintegrate what they have always been taught and what they have lately come to know through reflection, may we abandon the limits we have set up before now.

In its forth movement, this systematized apologetic must attempt to reply to those objections which are leveled at the very foundations of the act of faith.

Faith is vital knowledge, conscious life. The first conclusion to be drawn from all that we have said, therefore, is that it must progress ceaselessly, above all by penetrating to the significance of the Christian message, by extending its relationship to the whole of life, and by seeking depth and intimacy in communion of thought with the Lord.

VIII

Hope

CONTRARY to general opinion, the reality which we are about to consider is very complex. It is not unusual, therefore, to detect a certain inconsistency in the meaning attached to the word "hope" by many of the writers who treat of it. Our understanding of hope is as follows.

On the human level, hope has its roots in a twofold experience. A man becomes aware first that he wants a certain good; secondly, that he is relatively powerless to obtain it. He knows that he cannot obtain it of himself, but that he depends on exterior causes, and above all on the help of others.

On the religious level, hope is born when God promises man a good which lies in the future.

Hope is a dynamism, a movement towards happiness insofar as that happiness consists in union with God, and that the impulse towards it relies on God himself. Its unique complexity is

135

a result of the different levels on which this happiness is conceived, and in the different forms it takes, as well as on the different levels and forms of the divine promises which assure us of it.

1. GOD'S WORD

The Bible

The God of the Old Testament is he who takes care of his people. He guides them towards happiness and promises them his help and support. We can distinguish between three stages in the way in which God realizes and the people experience this support, which is the foundation of its hope. These three stages correspond to relationships between different levels of value.

In the first stage, happiness consists in the possession of the "land," and in the joy of living in this land united to God. There is at this stage a certain confusion between earthly and religious concepts of happiness.

During the second period, Israel has to learn to make a distinction between earthly happiness (on the economic and political levels), and religious happiness (which has its seat in the depths of the soul, and can exist even during the temporary absence of earthly joys). This trial of hope itself passes through two phases.

First, there is the Exile; the people are deprived of their land, but this deprivation is seen as a medicinal punishment; then follows the persecution for justice's sake, when God seems to abandon especially those who are faithful to him.

A third stage aims at a transformation of hope. The two levels of happiness, earthly and religious, fuse again into one, but in a transcendent way. Real synthesis is only possible by means of a "going beyond," and this in two ways. Each corresponds to an aspect of the trial. 1) After the Exile, the people of Israel return to their land, but this improvement in their situation does not, in fact, restore to them the good things which they had possessed in the days of their earthly glory. They must discover that, even in the penury of material goods, their life can be rich in that happiness which has its source in the interior presence of God. 2) When persecution brings about the death of the faithful of Yahweh, they must understand that victory over enemies and happiness are promised finally only for the next life which will be ours after death. Earthly goods are to be the object of our hope only insofar as they are related to eternal goods.

Here we find once again a fundamental law of the "plan of salvation," the law of the "way" by which God educates his people and unfolds progressively his revelation. God gives a first gift, still imperfect, which the people soon come to understand in too circumscribed and self-centered a way. Then God leads his people through a trial, by which their hearts are opened to go beyond their first conception; and God then gives them a more perfect gift.

We find, too, another law, a literary one this time, concerning the transformation in the meanings of the terms employed. New perspectives are expressed in the same terms as the old: blessing, land, kingdom, presence, and so forth, but these terms, now used in a changed context, have acquired a much more far-reaching significance.

Just as human "wisdom" is surpassed by the Wisdom given by the Lord, so too our human hopes receive from divine revelation both new perspectives and a firmer assurance; and men attain to these through conversion.

In this history of new-covenant hope, the role of the promised Messiah is important. But the ways in which this role is conceived correspond to the three successive ways of conceiving of the happiness which has been promised and the kind of help and support which will bring it about. Those Israelites who remained fixed in their hopes at a stage which they should have surpassed were not disposed to recognize the true Messiah. So when he came he was recognized only by the "poor of Yahweh."

The New Testament is at one and the same time the fulfill-ment of the promise of the Old Testament and the source of a new hope.

Jesus begins by bringing out the continuity between his mes-sage and the last stage of Old Testament wisdom: Blessed are the poor, for theirs is the kingdom of God. By the very fact of using this "wisdom-statement" in the present tense and in the context of the global proclamation "The kindom of God is at hand," Jesus declares that the hope of Israel is fulfilled in his coming, inasmuch as he is the Messiah who finally inaugurates the kingdom.

Then Jesus brings out the element of discontinuity, which de-mands a conversion. As much by his actions as by his words, he shows that the Messiah (King, as the viceroy of God in his kingdom) is not a political leader: and that earthly goods (given as miraculous signs and goods of the messianic order) are not distributed in such a way as to resolve all economic and social problems. Even on the religious level it is not to be expected that the "knowledge of God" will suddenly be made universal. On the contrary (and this, in fact, is directly in line with the Old Testament but with the least understood of its visions), the Messiah himself will have to suffer persecution because of his religious message.

Finally, Jesus proclaims his own particular revelation as going beyond all that came before and containing the foundation of a new hope. He reveals a higher order and gives a more perfect promise. The supreme good which he brings to men is union with God on a level hitherto unknown, the "knowledge" of God in his Son made man; happiness, "life," is "knowing you, who are the only true God, and Jesus Christ whom you have sent." The promise is above all existential. The gate of our hope (the living promise on which our hope rests) is the risen Christ who sends his Spirit.

Because of the importance of the promise in relation to hope, we will shortly study more particularly the promises made by Jesus; but first let us focus our attention on the development of the same "plan of salvation" which we met in the Old Testament. For Christ this plan consists in the paschal pattern of his existence: incarnation, death, resurrection. For the disciples of Christ this plan consists in a participation in the paschal way of Christ. Christian hope, as one element in the plan of salvation, has the same basic characteristics. Jesus himself showed an unwavering confidence in his Father; and perhaps the most remarkable feature in Christ's formation of his apostles is that he formed them above all to trust—that trust which clings to hope amidst all difficulties.

What, then, were the promises made by Christ?

The best way to know them is not to tie together in a miscellaneous bundle all those sayings from the Gospels which can be interpreted in the sense of promise. The Gospel has a profound unity, and the beams radiating from the center are understood in the radiance of that center. This center is the mystery of the death-and-resurrection. The central promise of Christ is the promise of his "return," of his "coming again."

This "return" of Christ takes place at different times and in different domains. The different ways in which the promises are to be understood correspond to the different ways in which the risen Christ is present among us—that is, 1) the victory of Christ over death and sin; the *resurrection* as his entry into the life of glory; and the manifestation of that life by his apparitions to the disciples; 2) our participation in the victory, which will one day be final, by our entry into *heaven;* eternal life will be fulfilled in the resurrection of the body; 3) the spiritual presence of Christ on earth, in his Church. This presence is active, and its *effects* are implied in promise.

Two questions arise here. First, where do we find this active presence? The answer is, through "mediations" of various kinds, especially the sacraments, prayer in common, authority, mutual charity.

Second, what kinds of effects are produced by these mediations of the promised presence of Christ? The answer: many effects, some absolute, some relative, according to the relationships between these different levels of existence.

The Liturgy

The sacraments are privileged "mediations" of the active presence of the Lord, pledge of our hope. This presence is realized in a unique way in the Eucharist. But this is not isolated from the other modes of his presence—such as the prayer of the assembly of the faithful.

The effects of the liturgical mediation belong absolutely to the theological sphere, and only in a relative way to the other spheres.

The liturgy is also the prayer-witness in which the community aspect of Christian hope is thrown into relief. Christians pray together for a hope which they share and which covers the happiness of all.

The sacraments, as well as the other liturgical prayers, show that sin is not an obstacle to hope. It is part of our actual human condition: it is one of the clearest signs of our needs of God's help, and victory over sin is precisely the object of our hope, the hope of all those who do not harden their hearts, but who are open to the promises of God.

The liturgical period of Advent has an eschatological dimension, but this includes certain earthly expectations which are also the object of our hope. Generally speaking, the prayer of petition is an application of hope, because it implies the expectation that we will receive what we ask for. We can even say that every prayer, and especially the prayer of praise and of thanksgiving, inasmuch as its accomplishment here on earth anticipates its eschatological fulfillment, is an exercise of the virtue of hope as it carries us on towards the perfect prayer of heaven.

Life Witness

The early Church bore splendid witness both to the pledge of eternal life which she received from the Holy Spirit, and of her own hope which was based on this pledge.

It might appear at first sight that since those early days the manifestation of Christian hope in the Church has diminished. A closer investigation forbids so absolute a judgment. It is true that the virtue of hope is lived imperfectly by the generality of her members: but she bears witness, always and especially today, to the pledge God has given her and to her own hope, in ways which perpetuate those of the early Christians, and develop them with new emphases.

So we have, then, lay men and women who are aware not only of their task of incarnating human values, but also of the exigencies of transcendence which this incarnation implies (this transcendence is itself based on hope); religious men and women whose way of life is essentially eschatological, and therefore based on Christian hope; and the Church as a whole, engaged in a conciliar life which in many spheres shows great vitality. This vitality is an effect of the pledge of eternal life communicated by the Holy Spirit, and the projects of the conciliar Church are full of hope.

Action, way of life, participation in the attitudes of the Church —all of these give their full light when they are interpreted, orally or in writing, by one whose vision is fully Christian. This is why it is important to consult Christian authors to see what Christian hope means to them.*

* A study from this point of view of the writings of Gabriel Marcel would be particularly rewarding.

Reflection and Formulation

The interpretation of the data of revelation and their application through tradition (and especially today) to thought and life, give rise to a double series of interconnected questions. One series of questions concerns the specific object of the act of Christian hope, and the other the characteristics of the act of hoping.

1. The object of Christian hope, in a word, is the gift which God has promised us in Jesus Christ. This gift first of all concerns eternal life, that is, heaven; it concerns also a new earth, that is, the resurrection of the body in a world appropriate to it; and last of all, it concerns a Christian death, that is, the final grace in the moment of death itself.*

This gift also concerns grace, which is often spoken of as a "means" to attain the final "end." For our part, however, without excluding completely the idea of a "means," we prefer to speak of it in terms of "mediation," for grace never works as a means pure and simple. Grace is "incarnated," lived in and through human activity, that is to say, in the realization of values, which are intermediary ends. Therefore, we have to take into account two complementary objects of Christian hope: grace as lived in the pursuit of religious values, that is, in actions which are explicitly referred to God; and grace as lived in the pursuit of secular values, that is, in actions which are implicitly referred to God.

Prayer, which is an action which explicitly refers to God, is not the only field of action of grace as lived in the pursuit of religious values. It acts also in every explicit witness to the faith, and in every witness of charity inspired by the love of God. Now, its effect, as far as hope is concerned, is precisely the growth of supernatural life, in ourselves and in others. This positive effect brings with it a twofold negative condition: a

* We consider these aspects of hope at greater length in our chapter on eschatology.

progressive victory over sin in our hearts, and the witness of good opposed to the scandal of evil which is ever renewed in the world.

The problem of the relationship between grace and profane secular values, calls for special prudence. When we treat of the theme of eschatology in a later chapter we will point out that the transformation of the human element by grace is achieved through an existential dialectic of continuity in discontinuity. This principle of action belongs to the very structure of the mystery of salvation.

We must also take into consideration two modes of mediation—two ways in which grace is incarnate. Of primary value are those which are anticipations of eternal life—for example, consecrated virginity—in which human values persist in sublimated form. Secondary are those which are preparations of the new (eschatological) earth—for example, the bodily fecundity of married couples—in which human values are lived as such, but also as signs (parables) to be transcended. In both cases there remain several factors which make for obscurity. We do not know exactly which mediations are in every case necessary, and we cannot be absolutely certain of them. Above all, we cannot foresee in detail the more-than-necessary which God will give us here on earth. It is better, moreover, that this should be so, for in this way our hope can live not by precise calculation, but by trust in God, who, in his goodness, goes beyond what we can foresee. This "going beyond" asks of us a conversion, since it replies to our desires "otherwise."

2. As for the act of hoping, we must now examine its elements, its qualities, and its conditions. Its constituent elements, for that is what we must consider first, are of four kinds. The first is the esteem of a value as the source of happiness—it is therefore of fundamental importance for Christian hope to have the greatest esteem for union with God, to consider it the supreme value and the ultimate happiness of man.

But there must also be in Christian hope a tension regarding the future, in view of a first realization of this hope, and above all in view of a growing and ever more perfect realization of one's hope. Christian hope tends towards a better realization of one's values—an ever increasing realization here below, and a perfect realization in the life to come.

Thirdly, there must be an awareness of our own helplessness to achieve this ultimate realization by our own power. Heaven will be a gift which we shall owe to the goodness of God. Grace, inasmuch as it is a progress towards this end, is also a gratuitous gift of God. Our sins, and the temptations which assail us from without and from within ourselves, are obstacles which we cannot overcome by our own powers alone. The radiation of salvation through the whole world is primarily a free act of God.

The last fundamental element of Christian hope is a certainty about the help of others, especially of the help of God himself. This certainty is based on our trust in the promise which God has given us of his help, the existential pledge in the resurrection of Christ producing its effect in the gift of the Holy Spirit, and also the verbal pledge contained in the most explicit promises.

Now, the corresponding qualities of the act of hoping are especially trust in whatever concerns the better realization of Christian values; a kind of audacity in the knowledge that one is helped and a humility in the knowledge that by oneself one is helpless; an energy that comes of the consciousness of the call of grace to action—action which grace also sustains, and also patience because the moment and the manner in which action will be effective depends above all on God, who judges thereof according to his own standards; and finally, fidelity, especially in moments of trial. For if hope gives the joy that comes of anticipation, it has also many dark valleys to cross.

Christian hope implies neither a flabby slackness, nor feverish hypertension, but firm tension in energy and patience. The confidence which animates it expects everything from God, even to expecting miracles, for our resurrection will be a miracle; but it also leaves to God all judgment as to what is opportune, and what is not.

Lastly, there are certain conditions for Christian hope, which are required so that the act of hoping can be born and develop normally. The first of these is a supernatural capacity which man receives through the infused virtue of hope. This virtue makes a man capable of assessing Christian values as a Christian, and of tending towards them.

A second condition is a certain interior disposition, a certain openness to supernatural values. This interior disposal is never perfect, which is why the dawn of hope in a soul and its progress demand a continual conversion.

Finally, there are certain conditioning psychological and sociological factors which at any rate influence the modality of the act of hoping. However, we shall discuss these at greater length in the following section.

Let us note here, nevertheless, the role which the "image" of the Church plays in the normal process of conditioning. Since the hope of a Christian is a participation in the Church, Christians must help each other to live their hope and to bear witness to it.

2. THE HUMAN BACKGROUND

The values in which man hopes to find his happiness form a whole which corresponds to the three basic needs of man: security, self-development, and communion. These three basic values, which are analogous to the three existential dimensions of man, are found under many different forms and in a number of combinations. Let us now try to distinguish what forms are most characteristic of the various age groups and sociological mentalities.

145

Psychology

Psychological conditionings, needless to say, influence all four constituent elements of the act of hoping. The first two—the esteem of a value and a tension about the future—are more concerned with the psychology of man considered as a being-in-process-of-becoming, who appreciates the values which he thinks will bring him joy, and who tends always towards the future.

A child lives in the present. He is generally less directed towards the future. He esteems the three basic needs or values of man in a confused kind of way, though his chief accent is own security.

The adolescent considers the two elements of esteem and tension above all from the point of view of the development of his personality. In seeking this development he experiences them analytically. The pre-adolescent, on the other hand, lives in the future, though in his dreams mainly, that is, by identifying himself with far-off heroes. At grips with the difficulties inherent in the awakening of the consciousness of liberty and of a greater instinctual vitality, the adolescent adopts generally as his horizon the more or less immediate future, when he hopes to attain greater self-command.

The adult is supposed to have achieved a certain integration of the three values, with his attention focussed especially on the construction of a better world by a realization of the present.

Regarding the final two elements, an awareness of our helplessness and a certainty in the help of others, the psychology here is more that of man as a dependent being, who must acknowledge his own weakness, and who is forced to rely on others.

In this respect, a child relies quite naturally on the people among whom he lives, and he normally trusts them. Sometimes these people destroy the child's trust by a hostile attitude, either manifest or concealed.

146

The adolescent, however, no longer wants to rely on others, but only on himself. Even so, he soon experiences his own weakness. Then he seeks the support of others, provided that he can in some way find himself again in them—for example, in the "gang" of one's own age group, or with the older friend who understands him and with whom he can discuss things.

Adults are called upon to rely on one another in a real community, structured in an appropriate sociological form of society.

Sociology

If we compare the three stages in the cultural expression of sociological conditions, we will find that, by and large, the accent is placed successively on the three basic values. Thus, in the "patriarchal" stage, the emphasis is on security in relation to the group and the land which belongs to the clan. In the "bourgeois" stage, values of interiorization and personal development take the upper hand. And finally, in the "technical" stage, the accent is once more, but differently, on the group, especially on the highly organized social body, and on the material bonds which assure its security.

Nevertheless, these emphases are not so simply made as it would appear in our breakdown, for a marked tendency in one direction often evokes in compensation a tendency in another direction. For example, in the modern world we can discern on the one hand a need for solidarity in organization, and on the other hand a desire for free encounter in a personalist community.

The other components of hope, however—anxiety about the future, the sense of personal weakness, dependence on others—are present in our modern world under conditions very different from those that existed in previous times.

Up until the end of the eighteenth century, man was only vaguely, if at all, interested in the future as containing important

147

change for this life on earth. He felt himself, especially in countries where life was still very close to the earth and nature, to be very dependent on mysterious forces which he was largely unable to control; he wanted to be able to lean on a god for support.

Our own times, on the other hand, are characterized by a consciousness of rapid evolution, in which man freely intervenes, with the result that he transforms his own condition by his own effort. This guided evolution (which on occasion takes form in revolution) is principally found on the technical and social levels. In both cases, it affects individuals, groups (or classes) of people, and nations. On the technical level, it is known as progress; on the social and political levels, the "advancement" of man that is essential. In particular, this advancement is considered essential of each individual in his relations with others (for instance, the advancement of women in society); that of workers in relation to management; and that of "young nations" with regard to "imperialism."

Thus in both of these domains wherein there lie the economic and social hopes of modern man, the individual has much more a feeling of existing as a "changing being" (that is, one oriented towards the future) and much less a feeling of living as a "dependent being" (that is, forced to depend confidently on the free action of others).

What influence do these social and technical changes have on the moral and religious domains? Once again, there arises the ambiguity of changes on the lower levels in relation to the higher domains.

If he reacts positively, modern man wants a morality in which the responsibility for judgment and the execution which rests with the conscience of each individual person in relation to his future situation are clearly manifest. He wants a religion, also, which has been rethought, thus allowing for a reinterpretation of traditional statements, and which is lived in community.

148

If, on the other hand, he reacts negatively, modern man rejects all forms of going beyond which involve an after-life and dependence on a Being who is superior to humankind.

This is why, today, an atheist's hope is one that falls back on itself. It develops in two directions at the same time: that of collective optimism which wants to be sure of itself but finds it hard to cover up its illusory hopes; and that of an existential pessimism which takes more account of the painful experiences of life against which the cynic is only able to reassure himself by voluntarily closing his eyes to the real possibilities offered by liberty and love. In both cases, this attitude is deprived of the dimension of immortality and the essential element of trust in him who is at once so different from us (for he is transcendent), and yet so close to us.

Christian hope in our own day must take in all the new human horizons on the economic and social planes insofar as they are related to the supernatural mystery of salvation. It will stress certain of its own aspects, for example that of the community, in connection with the good features in modern man's attitude.

3. COMMUNICATING THE MESSAGE

Preparation

We must base our catechesis on hope above all on the four constituent elements of hope.

1. The imparting of a Christian sense of values is part of the general task of all catechesis. Forming a person in faith as the Christian attitude of mind involves the imparting of an evangelical sense of values. One of the fundamental characteristics of this formation, however, is that catechesis must awaken in the catechized a desire for values. In relation to natural values, super-

natural values can be considered as their extension, though there is perforce discontinuity here, and though the supernatural virtues do in fact "go beyond" the natural virtues. They take flesh in the natural virtues, so to speak, only in order to elevate them, but this elevation can only take place through their being purified by a painful process of conversion. The power of the natural virtues to transcend themselves—and this power the supernatural virtues provides—is in some way linked with eschatological expectation. Therefore, when we speak of a pedagogy of the "beatitudes" as a pedagogy or way of teaching which answers the desire for happiness, we must be careful to take this process of conversion into account.

It must be recognized that the true appreciation of Christian values is only acquired by recognizing the relationship between the two levels of existence. This sense of value is nourished by meditation on and contemplation of these values in the life of Christ and in the lives of his faithful followers. To have a lively hope of heaven, one must ask God himself for a sense of values based on happiness, and happiness is being united with him, in Jesus Christ, with all his brothers.

The other components of hope also have a particular part to play in the catechesis of almost every subject, but taken together they comprise the subject matter of a special catechesis on hope. We will now consider them individually.

2. Hope means to involve oneself in the dynamic action of the mystery of salvation, that is, to stress the development of salvation in the future, to stress all that God wishes to bring about, to stress the cooperation that he expects of us.

3. Hope is the awakening of a consciousness of our weakness. It shows, that is to say, the emptiness of hope based solely on human effort, first because of man's natural weakness, and also because of his sinfulness. Sin is both a voluntary obstacle which man must now put aside, and a slavery which he is incapable of

throwing off without God's help. Humility, which recognizes our need of God, prepares us to receive his help in all its fullness.

4. Hope helps us to foster a recognition and use of the realities that support hope. God gives us his support by means of both the sacred and the profane, for his "mediations" are found in both. We must have recourse to the sacraments, to the prayer of intercession, and also to meditation on the promises, the pledges, and the help which God has already clearly given. We must seek this supernatural support through contact with the whole active and praying Church, as the "milieu of support" given to us by divine providence.

As regards natural aids, though they are not on the same plane as supernatural means of support, they normally form part of those conditions which favor the growth of Christian hope.

On all these points, it applies just as much to the other virtues as to hope that growth is dependent on exercise. Hope in particular is strengthened by faithfulness in the moment of trial.

Finally, we should take into account what is opposed to true hope. The means pointed out for fostering the first three constituent elements of hope aim at avoiding false hopes; those concerning the fourth contain the remedy for the temptation to despair, or at least for the lack of confidence in the future.

Procedure

We can in our catechesis ask the following series of questions, which correspond to the four constituent elements of hope.

1. What do you want of life? What, in your view, are the values which are important for happiness?

2. How do you think about the future? Hopefully? As including another life? With no hope? With no real concern?

3. What are the obstacles you see? Are they outside yourself? Within you? What do you think of death from the point of view of hope?

4. What is your hope based on? Is it based on a feeling of personal or collective strength? Is this sufficient to overcome all obstacles? Is it based on confidence in the good will of other men? On the power and goodness of God? On the promises of Christ? On the guarantees of the Spirit in the Church?

Hope of a general kind is the hope for happiness, success, a life lived to the full. But what are the things of value which will give us happiness? What does success consist in? At what levels are happiness, success, and fullness of life to be found? As regards human hopes, the underfed and the poor hope for better material conditions of life—for food, for money, which secures the material needs of life. The weak want to become strong and important, healthy, educated. Those who are suffering from domination, oppression, and exploitation hope for liberation, which will give them liberty and the chance for social advancement. The person who, even though he has material well being and social liberty, feels lonely, neglected, and deprived of affection, wants to love and be loved.

Christian hope concerns itself specifically on the supernatural level with the life to come, and, on earth, with its anticipation. We hope for heaven, which is the perfect realization of charity; we hope in the kingdom of God, the new earth, which will fulfill and surpass all our efforts to build a better world. We hope to live, already on earth, more and more in union with God, and to radiate his love to men. One of the most effective ways of radiating this love is to be found in voluntary poverty, in the service of the apostolate. We hope for a progressive victory over sin, for the growth of the Church, which is the community of all men in Jesus Christ.

Finally, hope draws all its strength from supernatural sources, but it takes flesh on earth in human hopes—its "mediations"—which it raises to a higher level. Hope, then, is the virtue of the wayfarer, of the person "on his way." It is the virtue of progress towards perfect communion in Jesus Christ, in which the kingdom of God is realized, bringing with it the salvation and happiness of men. Hope goes forward praying. Its simplest and deepest prayer is the "Our Father."

IX

Charity

1. GOD'S WORD

The Bible

THE most holy God comes to meet man in his benevolent and merciful love. God creates man as persons with whom he personally enters into contact. When men refuse to respond to God's love, he manifests the most astonishing quality of his charity, that is, his mercy. This is the great message of the prophets about the covenant which Yahweh concluded with Israel, his child, his spouse, his vine, his people to whom he gives a new heart. Love's reply, summarized in the "schema" of the old love, will be given in its perfection by the "Servant of Yahweh" who brings us salvation.

The Messiah, sent by God, is his Son made man. Jesus ac-

155

complishes his task, simply and concretely, by living in charity. He receives the Father's perfect love, and responds to it with faultless faithfulness. The Father desires of him that he work for our salvation.

Jesus does this in three ways. First, he proclaims, in deed and word, what God does for his people out of love for them. By dying, secondly, he makes reparation for our sins: greater love than this no man has. Finally, glorified in the sight of the Father, he passes on to the Church his life and his power of loving, by sending to her the Holy Spirit.

Moreover, when his "hour" was come, Jesus gave us an essential directive, that we love each other as he had loved us; this loving will effect in us a "radiation" of divine charity, wherein the Son is united to the Father and wherein we are united to him.

The writings of the apostolic times describe this experience of the Church, which, as Christ's community, then as now lives in charity "on the march" towards perfect union.

St. Paul says that charity is the "gift" most sublime and most necessary, and that we must live in it as Jesus himself did. We see by the rebukes that Paul addresses to them, however, that this charity was not practiced by the early Christians without difficulty and failings.

For St. John, the Christian attitude is expressed in "one" commandment: belief in God (that is, response to his love), together with love of one's neighbor (that is, the most practical way of making the love of God a reality, a love of the God "whom we do not see" by taking up the truly Christian attitude towards our fellow men "whom we do see").

The Liturgy

Forming a "community of prayer," the liturgy teaches us charity in the most outstanding way. The Eucharist expresses and gives effect to the gift of ourselves to God along with Christ. It is a

156

personal gift in communion with the whole Church, in such a way that our encounter with God bears as its fruit the union of all Christians among themselves. To be sure, Christians celebrating the Eucharist are still very imperfect men, and even sinners. But prayer as a community teaches them to overcome the opposition unavoidable at a lower level, and to reach understanding on the level of more sublime values.

This union in God then spreads abroad light and strength to promote a harmonious life in community as well as in ordinary human spheres.

Life Witness

A Christian who truly loves God and his neighbor for God's sake, shows his charity in actions. It will, therefore, be possible in catechesis to make use of the witness of Christians, by taking examples from family life, cases of mutual help, and so forth. But ordinary examples do not always solve the problem of detecting in what way Christian behavior presupposes a motive force of charity different from a love of one's neighbor as it is practiced by non-Christians. What we are looking for, in fact, are the signs of a charity which is a theological virtue. Indeed, it is possible that theologal charity may be at work "incognito" (in an implicit way) in mutual help between non-Christians. But what directly concerns catechesis are the signs of the charity which comes from God and goes back to God in order to radiate from there upon all men, signs which are as explicit as possible.

Such *explicit* witness is to be found in Christians who have a clearer experience of it, and who have given open expression to the fact that the power of their charity came from God, as a gratuitous sharing in the charity that animates the life of Jesus Christ.

People who have given themselves to a greater extent to the

apostolate, and others concerned more directly with the basic tasks of human life but faithfully nourishing their spiritual lives on prayer, do in fact experience a call to a charity which transcends the mere framework of life. With this call, which has its special expression in the Gospels, such people receive the promise of a power of charity which unites them in a special way to Christ. They draw this power in particular from the sacraments, knowing that God is concerned at every moment with upholding and sustaining them. In their practice of charity towards their neighbor, moreover, they are not seeking for honor and glory in the eyes of men, and still less for self-satisfaction; they remain humble because what they do always falls short of the divine appeal. This is so even when what they do considerably exceeds what one can normally expect of a man. St. Vincent de Paul, for example, was humbly aware that his love and work for the poor was only a beginning; yet his effort was heroic.

An analogous type of witness to that of the love of God expressed in works could be found in the lives of those who, above all, express the love of God in contemplative communion.

Reflection and Formulation

If charity has not always been given its central position which falls to it by right, in statements of Christian doctrine, the renewal in moral theology has now given it a more prominent place.

But any thinking of the sapiential type in particular on charity needs to be constantly renewed, refined, and linked with the way in which man here and now is thinking about his life and his activities. The data needed for developing such a line of thought at the present moment should come in the second part of our considerations: the attitude of man as a result of his psychological development and sociological conditioning. However, at this point it seems preferable to develop this *anthropological* line of thought in order to prepare the way for a theological consideration which is necessary for a proper understanding of revelation and for the presentation of the Christian mystery of charity in catechesis.

1. THE ASPECTS OF LOVE

It is commonplace to say that the word "love" has many very different meanings, and indeed, some of them are quite contradictory. These latter, however, are only tendential excesses which must be brought to reconciliation, if by no other means, at least by a dialectical balance in the rhythm of life.

• We all begin loving by being loved, and the first aspect of love (love, that is to say, as a dynamic force which creates values) is that which is directed towards the subject itself: this is *interested love*. It is the synonym of "love born of desire" or "love of possession" (though on several levels).

We have already met with this kind of love in our discussion of hope, with which it is sometimes confused. It is only one of its components, however, together with others which are not essential to all love. Hope also, as part of its make-up, has the element of "distance." In the first place, there is the distance of time: the man who hopes has not yet got what he hopes for. This factor of distance is partially overcome by the foretaste of possession: man already has the pledge. There is also the element of distance between persons: man hopes of others (or at least with the help of others) what he is incapable of realizing by himself. For the man who hopes to receive, this distance is conquered by confidence in the person who gives, especially by confidence based on that person's former promise. Thus hope is the moving towards the realization of values, above all the value which fulfills the sum of all desires. Now, there is still one

159

further discovery to be made before the most important value of all can be realized.

The search for values must reveal a further double aspect of love.

• When he reaches a certain strength, a man finds himself equally capable of giving help to others in their need. The person who has had the experience of trusting others, now experiences their putting trust in him.

The love directed towards others for their sakes, *disinterested love,* finds its expressions mainly in the "love of service."

• The most important value with which a person can wish to come into contact dwells in another person; and in its fullness, in all other persons. Now, this discovery transforms the concepts of interested and disinterested love.

Interested love going out to a person cannot be a possessive love which subordinates the other person to myself, which makes of the other a mere means to an end which is identified with myself. The other person has a right to respect. He has a right to be himself. I cannot deprive him of his liberty. Interested love must then become one of respect for and acceptance of the other person. This kind of love makes of the beloved what he really is: "I love him because he is who he is."

On the other hand, disinterested love, which tends to lead to the forgetting of self, cannot be conceived in such a way as to make contact with the other person become impossible, mainly by a process of self-effacement by the person who should make contact with the other. Disinterested love must always bear in mind, therefore, that it is the love of a living interpersonal relationship.

Purified of their possible excesses, these two aspects of love become one by transcending themselves in an activity in which they intercommunicate. This intercommunication is not necessarily one of equality or uniformity or relationships one way or the other, but an activity consisting of mutual gift. The great discovery is, in fact, that the person is capable of giving himself to another person and of receiving the gift which the other person makes of himself to him: this is *communional love,* or the love of communion.

We are now in the position to discuss what we might call the "cross currents" of these aspects of love. Disinterested love can concentrate its attention to such an extent on others that the person forgets himself. Now, as this kind of love is one of the most difficult things to achieve, practical considerations of love are usually concerned with it in particular. It is emphasized that self-renunciation is necessary in order to love others. Attention is drawn to the nobility of this act of self-denial done in the service of one's neighbor, that is, towards whom the person who loves has to "lower" himself the most in order to come to his help. This love takes on its most perfect forms when it does not wait for the one in need to call upon it: in particular, when it is the creator of others: it is love that gives life, that is to say, which makes others live when they did not yet exist, either physically or on some value level.

However, when love does all this, it acts in virtue of a personal capacity, and all normal exercise of such a capacity is the cause of joy. Furthermore, those who witness the action—and in the first place the person who benefits from it—are led to recognize the power, the goodness, and the nobleness of the person who helps others. It redounds to his honor, the meriting of which is equally a source of joy. This means that pure disinterestedness is an abstract concept.

In actual practice, help generally takes the form of mutual assistance. This means that there normally lies behind any act of service an acceptance of the "rules of the game" in the social domain. All men must help one another. The person who helps others expects to be helped in his turn when he finds himself in

F

need. The most frequent kind of mutual help is directed to the joint winning of common advantages, and this solidarity can give rise to a number of additional problems when it is called upon to place itself at the service of another group.

It remains true, on the other hand, that disinterestedness can on occasion reach heroic heights. Can it lead to death, go to the point of accepting total loss of self? For the person who is conscious both of the value of each individual person and of his immortal destiny, the answer is in the negative. What, then, must we say of the person who gives his life, the man who, that is to say, renounces his earthly existence? This brings up the whole problem of the relationship between individuals and the community.

We can only deal with the matter briefly here, however. On the purely material level, the individual member of society is sometimes called upon to do away with himself for the good of the whole, that is, of the majority—or rather, the whole as realized in a new way. On the spiritual plane, no individual person stands to gain from another doing away with himself out of charity; on the contrary, every person gains from being himself to the fullest possible extent, and from entering into active contact with others. The abandoning of earthly life for the sake of others, therefore, finds its meaning and has limits imposed upon it in and by the situation of man in this world, in and by the opportuneness of material "mediations," and in and by his transitory state as he journeys towards eternity.

Self-denial has no absolute value in itself; it is a phase in the movement which leads to communion.

It is in this sense, adopted by the mystery of salvation that the two complementary statements of Jesus must be understood, ones which he himself put into practice in a most outstanding way: "Greater love has no man than to lay down his life . . . I lay down my life in order that I may take it up again." Once again, we meet the unique mystery of "cross and resurrection."

In this light, we can make out more clearly the relationship between love and *sacrifice*. The origins of sacrifice are religious: it arises from a desire to show recognition of God and to be united with him. Several theories have laid stress on somewhat misleading interpretations, for example that of destruction, when it is important to remember the essential of religion which is good, a communion. The journey towards union is made in two stages: man must abandon all that keeps him apart from God, and he must accept to be taken up by God in a union. Analogically, sacrifice will characterize love between human persons; one party must be ready to abandon not only a selfishness which is opposed to the interests of the other party, but even all exclusive possession, in order to place everything in common in mutual communion.

Renunciation as such, of course, is ordered to the full flowering of the person by the transcending of self in the encounter with others. A purely spiritual communion presents less difficulties than the "sharing in communion" of the "mediations" of love. This latter can never be complete. Besides, it is only to be sought in proportion as it fosters the union of the persons themselves.

"Love of communion," insofar as it is not completely realized, and is dependent on others, is also the object of hope. As Gabriel Marcel has said, "I hope in you for us."

Finally, communion is not to be identified with equality. We shall take up this matter later on, however.

2. THE PSYCHIC MAKE-UP OF PERSONALITY

Love is called upon to penetrate all the layers of personality, starting with what is deepest and most interior, and going right through what is exterior and most communicable. This is achieved by a reciprocal influence: exterior help given by others would not be charity if it were not inspired by interior sincerity; a deep desire only achieves its true fullness through an adequate form of expression.

In fact, the awakening of a "personal" love, as with that of liberty, starts from without. The exterior part of man's make-up, his body, is also the seat of his experiences and reactions in which his inner liberty is involved. For example, the expression of love between the mother and her child involves the deeper part of the mother's adult personality in a different way from the child's as yet underdeveloped personality. In the mother, her love for the child, expressed in her care for him, can be the expression of a love which involves her entire liberty, whereas in the child, his attachment to the person who cares for him will at first only be an immediate exterior reaction (physical proximity) set off by a vital instinct without the awakening of personal liberty. But with the awakening of his deeper powers and their development, the child will recognize in his mother's attitude and that of the people whom he meets, the "*signs*" *of a love* which lives in them *at a level deeper than instinct.*

The progressive awakening of the various layers of personality concerns in particular *affective love,* which is love looked at from within. It exists on the level of the senses as physical attraction; on the emotional level, as emotive love; in the affective element at its deepest level, it is found in respect for the person.

Another distinction concerns *effective love* in particular. This is love taken from the point of view of its expression. Man expresses himself in three ways: by external actions, by symbolic gestures, and by words. Love is expressed by service rendered, or by an act of practical obedience, by a kiss, by a gesture expressing admiration, or by conversation (dialogue).

One must avoid unduly restricting definitions and terms or considering as identical realities which have between them only a certain affinity. Thus interested love is related to the affective aspect, and this is on the emotional level; while disinterested love concerns itself with the effective side, and this takes a practical form. But it is certain that complete love, the love which brings about "personal" communion, presupposes the affective element at its deepest, and the appropriate form of expression, of which dialogue or even silence when it is highly meaningful, is sometimes the most penetrating and purposeful form.

Interior and exterior—and in this sense affective and effective —love must possess two moral qualities which characterize all interpersonal relationships: sincerity and fidelity.

It remains for us to see how interpersonal relationships take a number of different forms, and this diversification introduces a large number of divisions into love.

3. DEVELOPMENTS OR DIVISIONS OF LOVE IN INTERPERSONAL RELATIONSHIPS

We have already analyzed the aspects of love seen from the point of view of the subject seeking his own good, that of others, or communion of goods. These aspects which constitute all complete love when taken together and considered in terms of the direction, present a different series of facts.

We can distinguish, therefore, between love which "goes up" to someone who is superior in the sense that he can help, that one admires him; love which "goes down" to those who are in need; and love which "moves on the same level," though this in itself takes a multiplicity of forms.

Either people seek and find in one another what is complementary to each, as in the case of sexual partners; or they find their union in mutual understanding, in the deeper domains of personality which call for a certain degree of psychological penetration, as in the case of friends; or they feel a solidarity in their pursuit of the same objective which lies outside their interpersonal communion, as in the case of companions in work, in

games, in cultural activity, in war. The biological basis for this
type of solidarity is consanguinity between brothers and in its
farthest extension between all men. From the "personal" point
of view, it reaches its zenith in a community of destiny which
consists precisely in the most perfect communion possible between all men.

We can also distinguish, therefore, love which breaks through
disunions. It can do this in several ways. It can break through
psychological barriers: the love of strangers. It can break through
in the case of breaches in relationships which are regretted: the
love which pardons. It can, finally, break through in the case of
oppositions which still exist, when these do not affect the roots
of personality itself, or when they have not taken on a permanent character. This is the love of enemies. Enemies are men
opposed to one another on a particular level of "mediation," but
they remain people with whom we are called upon to preserve
the possibility of unity at deeper levels.

According to whether the person takes the initiative himself
or responds to the initiative of others, the love will be either
spontaneous and free or a returned love born of gratitude. However, it should be remembered that in the dialogue of communion
the initiatives are being continuously reversed following a more
or less regular rhythm.

Of course, in the majority of cases several of these divisions
of love integrate with one another more or less perfectly.

4. THE TERMINOLOGY OF LOVE AND CHARITY

We wish here to summarize our terms. They are: interested and
disinterested love, and communional love; love of possession and
the love of respect and acceptance (complaisance); love of
service; love of communion; affective love and effective love;
love between complementary partners, between friends, between

companions. Other authors writing on the subject of love use different terms which, however, link up with the ones above, though on occasion with different associations. Thus for some writers erotic love is equated with interested love; the love of desire with the love of concupiscence; for others, sexual love means emotional, not physical, love.

In the same way, the word "friendship" can be used either of all love which is not simply the "love of desire," or, as we have used it, of the love based on a mutual understanding at the level of personality.

Finally, we must distinguish uses of the word "charity." This must not be reduced to a mere "beneficial love," or a "service rendered," or an "act of kindness," or in general "philanthropy." There are two sides to the meaning of the word as we use it: disinterested love, and love based on communion which integrates by transcending both interested and disinterested love.

2. THE HUMAN BACKGROUND

We have already discussed the human background to love-charity which is applicable to all men. Now we must attempt to throw further light on those aspects of man's conditioning which result specifically from psychological and sociological differences.

Psychology

Differences of temperament and of cast of mind are related to differences in the psychic area. Minds which stress *continuity,* that is, what men share in common, think of charity mainly in terms of mutual help—and this mutual help itself is thought of more in terms of the application of a law of society and on a rather uniform and egalitarian basis. On the other hand, those who are more aware of *discontinuity,* that is, the unique element in each

167

person, think of charity more particularly in terms of interpersonal communion: and this communion in terms of a living dialogue which respects differences and which constitutes a pluralist and complementary unity.

This difference occurs again together with others when we look at different temperaments. For example, there are very great temperamental differences in the masculine and feminine psychologies alone. A man more easily aims at an effective charity in organized acts of mutual help; a woman, on the other hand, will be more sensitive to affective charity going out to each person in a unique way. This is the basic direction, of course, and again, it is not uncommon for there to take place, and there should indeed take place, an integration of affective and effective charity in both men and women. It is important to avoid an oversimplified picture as if ·a man were all efficiency and a woman all emotion; in fact, the deep affective element in a man expresses itself more naturally in social actions; and the very lively devotion of a woman to the person of others is more often emotional in character.

The development of a psychological attitude towards others taken as a whole follows the general pattern of psychological development. This pattern falls into three main stages: confused awareness (unity without distinction), confrontation (distinction without unity), and integration (unity with distinction).

The three phases of the rhythm will turn up an indeterminate number of times in the course of development. In childhood, however, it will be the aspect of confused awareness which predominates, that of confrontation in adolesence, and in (psychological) adulthood that of integration.

One can easily see that it is the "confrontation" stage which sets the clearest and most numerous problems. The ways which will lead on from the state of confused awareness are already outlined in *childhood*. One can, in fact, teach a child to be grateful (to show "recognition," that is, the recognition that others are good for him), or to share with his fellow creatures—"taking turns" in play, for instance, can have an important part in this development; or to indulge in the admiration of others.

The *pre-adolescent* develops his ability to admire, but he uses it to identify himself temporarily with some rather distant heroes; these identifications are merely successive attempts to discover himself. For in all that concerns those whom he sees as different from himself, he prefers to keep them at a distance, and before long he begins to oppose them. At first, this opposition is directed against those who wish to impose themselves on him in virtue of established authority; there then follows opposition to all those who obstruct his desire (which has become by now a psychological necessity) to act on his own, to be himself. The "gang" still serves to give him a feeling of power, but it will not be enough, and will not last.

This is because the *adolescent* goes through the inevitable and normal experience of having to make a "choice," and he experiences many prior orientations before making this choice, and many consequences. The most important choice of all consists precisely in that of deciding whether priority is to be given to others or to self. The first possible choice, of course, is the priority of self; this is a slipping back into self-centeredness, from which the discovery of others should free him. The second possibility: priority of others. As an adolescent, who sees everything in terms of black and white, goes spontaneously from one extreme to the other, at least in his demands, he will look upon this choice in absolute and altruistic terms. He will devote all his energies to a thing in order to become capable of doing it. But disappointing experiences, both with regard to his own efforts and to what he sees around him, destroy this illusion. Once again, there is a danger of returning to self-centeredness. Hence it is supremely important for the adolescent, particularly now, to discover charity as communion. This marks the beginning of an integration which will take a long time, but which is the right solution and the one to be aimed at. This "forward-looking" solution will be seen as the quickest and most obvious one when a person in whom the adolescent is ready to confide helps him to recognize that all experiences in our relationships with others find their meaning in that they form part of the process which leads to communion. This development, finally, takes place in an analogous way in the multiform aspects of love: in the family, in sex, in working in company with others, and so forth.

Sociology

Human experiences, even those which seem to involve no one but the individual concerned, always take place in an environment and are related to that environment. In fact, the influences of several environments are at work at the same time, especially in the case of charity, which is of its nature an experience of relationships with others.

1. THE EDUCATIONAL ENVIRONMENT

This environment plays a leading role in the early years. If at home and at school a child has normal experiences in regard to relationships which are the basis of charity, he will be more receptive to the revelation of God's love and better disposed to respond to it. If he is "spoiled," he runs the danger of becoming wedded to undeveloped forms of love. If, on the contrary, he finds himself "frustrated," he will seek compensations. This can take place in two opposite directions: either that of religious sentimentality, which is to say, where he withdraws into his natural affectivity and tends to turn religion into self-centered sentimentality; or that of sublimation, where he welcomes supernatural charity and wants to make it shine out in all his relationships with others.

170

2. THE MODERN ENVIRONMENT

The modern environment is characterized by two opposite and complementary tendencies with regard to charity. First and foremost, man has a keen sense of universal solidarity in the social sphere and of a power given us by our technical civilization of raising the standard of living everywhere. This sense can have one of two effects. Either it encourages the putting into practice of social charity on a large scale, or the great temptation arising from this keen consciousness rears its head in this first tendency in the form of a desire to show that men have no need of God in order to find happiness together on earth.

The other tendency, on the contrary, is born of the modern experience of the state of powerlessness in which men find themselves, an inability really to live as a person with others. In reaction against the hold taken by organization following in the wake of technical progress, the desire "freely to be oneself" is taken to its extreme. Henceforth, it becomes impossible to approach others as free agents; and they for their part can be nothing other than a threat to the development of one's own freedom. The man who has banished God from his life, no longer knows what it means to love; he says love is impossible and life absurd.

These two tendencies manifest within themselves a need of reorientation, and thus bring to light the immediate importance of Christian charity. In a world which is moving towards unity at all levels, Christians must practice charity in the most effective way possible. A charity which is really concerned with social justice and enlivens it with a higher principle, the principle of "life from above" (superanimation) which is also the principle of healing and one which, at the same time as it gives support, calls for a conversion. Christian charity in the modern world will have to move more definitely in the direction of furthering the material well being of all men; but this must be done without overlooking their happiness in the life hereafter, but rather in carrying out this work with a true sense of proportion resulting from the fact that it is related to a hope for eternal happiness and depends on the supernatural values which characterize it. Finally, in the actual preparation for this charity which is only to attain its full flowering later on, Christian charity is already explicitly communional in character on earth. Its desire is to secure the good of all men, but it puts their happiness less in the "possession" of material and cultural riches than in "ways of being" and in particular "being with." Charity is the actual living of interpersonal relationships.

Faced with the other tendency which must be counteracted (that tendency which leads those people to despair who no longer know what "personal" love is, and who therefore say it is impossible), Christian witness must bring to the forefront the signs of that charity already lived in reality, even though imperfectly. It must go further than the signs which men give one another on their own human level. The Christian message is, in fact, that of divine charity which has "appeared" to us in Jesus Christ and is "communicated" by the Holy Spirit.

Charity is more than just a problem. It is a mystery which is beyond our powers of understanding, but whose meaning we grasp better and better in proportion as we open ourselves up to its actions, and as we cooperate with it.

3. COMMUNICATING THE MESSAGE

Preparation

It is possible, at least implictly, to put all the essentials of charity into a *very simplified* catechesis. For example: The love of God must consist more in deeds than in words. The deeds which matter most are acts of charity towards one's neighbor, for it is in this way that we prove our love of God by obeying his great commandment; and thus we put into practice our love for Jesus Christ, whom we meet in our neighbor.

However, a moment's reflection will suffice to make one aware of the danger contained in a simplification of this kind. It is the tendency which makes itself felt keenly especially nowadays—to "reduce" the love of God to the love of one's neighbor; to confuse the love of God and the love of neighbor as a result of a mind framework which leads to pantheism or to atheism (as in the case of Buddhism); to suppress the vertical dimension in love for the sake of its horizontal dimension.

In order to avoid this danger, it is important that the catechist himself at least should have a clear enough idea of the kind of connection that exists between the love of God and the love of one's neighbor. The latter is normally dealt with for the first time as part of pre-catechesis. At a second stage, that of catechesis properly so called, the object is love as concerned with God directly in person. At a third stage, the teacher should devote himself to showing how the love of God shines out through love of one's neighbor.

The second of the above three stages should be dealt with as soon as the opportunity presents itself, and it should be taken up again and progressively developed to the fullest extent possible, because it is the very core of religion. In fact, the Christian mystery is first and foremost the mystery of love which God brings to us in Jesus Christ, and which is communicated to us by the Holy Spirit; the Christian mystery is next that of universal brotherly love, but this as the response to God's love and the putting into action of God's gift.

A *developed* catechesis of the love of God should be built within the framework of love seen as an encounter, God having the initiative in it. The full meaning of this initiative and that of the response to be given it only becomes clear slowly through progressive development.

The historical development should be used here in order to show the signs of the love which God has for us.

Any teaching of charity presupposes a careful teaching of faith because we first have *to believe in the love which God shows for us* (1 Jn. 4, 16). Our response to the manifestation of God's love does not immediately attain the perfection of a love of the same kind as God's. For a great many men, God is quite simply the all-powerful Sovereign Master who dispenses gifts to men. They are not slow to understand that it is their duty to love God with *a love born of admiration and gratitude,* but this attitude goes hand in hand with a certain dread of the holy, because naturally man fears all power which is not under his control. His predominating concern thus becomes that of keeping the commandments of the all-powerful Master and of warding off his anger when he transgresses them. The greatness of God also calls for praise, but the worship in which this praise would find its expression is reduced on occasion to the mere observance of ritual laws.

Catechesis will help in the making of the first steps towards a faith in God's love, by stressing the goodness and kindness of God who deserves all our *confidence.* We can expect of God gifts of increasing number and size.

Often, an objection will here be raised as a result of the evil in the world and the apparent state of abandonment in which God leaves man. The answer to this objection demands a certain purification of our ideas and our desires. In brief, what must we expect from God?

The teaching of faith in love links up with that of hope in love. The teaching of charity must here make use of the "dialectical" approach.* which is essential in order to discover the relationship which exists between human hopes and Christian hope.

Progress in charity works on the basis of the same fundamental

* See Chapter 1, "Catechesis: Its Triple Task," in *The Structure of Catechetics,* pp. 12–21.

dialectic which governs the tension between the more human realities and divine realities. This law makes as much for the understanding of God's love for us as for our commitment in our love to God.

With regard to the first element of the encounter, recognizing God's love for us, one can show that his love has that quality of "otherness" in the same way as his justice has. All love calls for an acceptance based on the free response of others. God calls upon us as free agents. God's good will has our progress in mind. This is why every gift of God is ordered to furthering progress, not necessarily quantitively but certainly qualitatively: by his first gifts God prepares us for higher ones. But the acceptance of a higher gift carries with it the acceptance of the correspondingly higher demands. For example, when God shows us a love which is ready to forgive those who have offended him, he calls upon us to be ready to forgive the men who have offended us. It is a call to conversion. *Man only advances in his knowledge of the love of God as he becomes converted.*

This is also true in the strictly religious domain, before applying it to charity towards one's neighbor. God's love for us takes flesh first of all in the earthly realities which God uses as parables. In every parable we have to see its inner meaning, we have to go beyond it. This calls for detachment.

The *trial*s of love in which the "relative" character of the human parables of divine charity stands out more clearly, the absence of certain of our joys, the voluntary renouncements of one or other of the earthly forms of love, have an educative part to play in opening us up to God's love. Deprivation is one of the stages in the (dialectic) struggle leading to a higher realization of love; one must avoid just as much making it loom too large as neglecting its importance. This is what all the saints have realized in practice and all spiritual writers who have mapped out the road by which a man comes to a recognition of God's love for him and to the point where he responds to it.

The catechesis of the second element in the encounter—witnessing to our love for God—will also have to follow a dialectical development, first on the anthropological level, that of pre-catechesis, and then on the theological level, that of catechesis.

The teaching of a love which answers God's love will benefit by creating awareness insofar as possible of those things which go to make up all love. Thus already in pre-catechesis one is concerned with discovering that the love of others is a cause of joy in us as a result of feeling ourselves to be loved, and thus we are called upon to correct our latent selfishness. The human experience of love educates us in confidence as well as in generosity. The person who is loved knows that the love of others gives him great strength, both psychologically and morally; and he knows that even with this strength, faithfulness to the gift of himself often and repeatedly becomes difficult.

The catechesis which takes over from this pre-catechesis will thus underline that God's love for us brings us more than mere psychological strength; God gives us the Holy Spirit who acts in us and with us in order that we may be able to love God in return in a far higher way than we can through mere human effort. At the same time, this catechesis will make clear the demands that the setting in motion of this power carries with it, for our love of God must take flesh in acts of obedience and service in the interests of God. This service, however, will not simply be a labor whose weight bears us down. It will be a joyous activity expressing our love of communion with God.

The whole structure of love conceived as an encounter between God and man can be seen in a striking light in Jesus Christ, a light which on earth remains enveloped to a certain extent in darkness, with the result that the darkness seems to prevail at times over the light. This is one more reason for taking great care in catechesis when dealing with the signs of his love, which God

176

gives us in Jesus Christ, and with signs of the response which he expects of us as we follow in Christ's footsteps.

A catechesis worked on this basis should result by the grace of God, in a renewal and furthering of living faith in the love in which we are united to God. It is of the first importance that the catechist should help, by all the means at his disposal, those entrusted to him to awaken within themselves a truly personal love of God, a love that will radiate in a generous love of neighbor. A personal love is nourished by a deep conviction: God loves me personally, really and much more deeply than I can understand. His love reveals itself to me in all its brilliance in Jesus Christ. God loves all men; he leads them all to the discovery and fulfillment of a complete communion. My loving of God is my most important job in life: the one which embraces and inspires above all else that I have to do. By the grace and power of the Holy Spirit, I am capable of loving him every day more and more. I am called to live in communion with him, to work with him so that at one and the same time I can show him my love and cooperate with him in spreading his love throughout the world. A similar conviction of faith in God's love together with the driving force of *hope in the progress of our charity* will sustain the very growth of love through the most difficult periods as in moments when our hearts are filled with a human joy. For the love of God comes to life through every "mediation."

Procedure

As for the form of presentation to be used in this teaching, the suggestions which seem to us most called for are related to the three qualities demanded of a balanced progression.

First of all, emphasis should be judiciously put on all the points which correspond to the stage which has been reached in psychological development, and this stressing should be completed at least by a discreet glimpse at the other components of charity.

Thus with *children* the starting point will naturally be the image of a father's love, and one will have to lead the child beyond this so as to receive the love of our Father in heaven. When the child has undergone some unhappy experience in family life, the revealing of God's love will serve as a compensation for the frustration met with on the earthly level, but this compensation cannot be presented as something to be found on the same level. A child can at a very early age "start" to commit himself to a kind of love which is essentially one of "mystery."

In the case of *adolescents,* there is an awakening desire for a love of a kind which is clearly more personal and which involves the emotions. The emphasis which suits them is one which leads to their recognizing something which sets people on fire, in the love that Jesus has for each individual (calling each of his disciples in a way specially suited to each apostle) . . . but also they must be led to see that they are called upon to go beyond mere emotional sympathy in their love. For young people, the love of Christ is the quickening of life at a deep level through a task being shared by him and ourselves in the human community.

Two needs of charity are felt by *adults* who experience life to the full in their own "environments"; the demand for social efficiency, that is, for taking action with regard to conditions in order to better man's lot; and the desire for a personal encounter based on fidelity. Catechesis will answer their hopes by transcending them. In the first place, it will point out that these two desires are complementary and that the first must be placed at the service of the second; this already constitutes a breakthrough on the human level. Another breakthrough on this same level has to be brought about in regard to self-centeredness in personal contacts with others. Finally, the main breakthrough is the one to divine charity which shines out over all mankind. The love of

God is the "divine milieu" which must penetrate and impregnate all human environments and which invites us to transcend them once and for all in a way whose fulfillment, by passing through death, has as yet only been revealed to us in its principle. This principle is a living one; it is the risen Christ, living in the fullness of the Holy Spirt.

In the second place, we must in our catechesis encourage through a joy which communicates itself by a call for generosity and patience.

Christian charity offers quite enough wonderful expressions of itself lived joyfully (for example, missionaries, converts, ordinary Christians whom we meet every day), for it to be possible to arouse a generous and confident desire for a charity which goes beyond mere lukewarmness. But the journey to the heights is not accomplished by one single effort; it calls for patience over a long period which is a form of humility, for it recognizes that our strength and its growth come from God.

Finally, it is the duty of catechesis to place the teaching of charity in the existential framework of real commitments.

Teachers must not restrict themselves to moralizing about the practice of charity in given frameworks: at home, at school, and so forth. They must also help and encourage efforts which need to be made in voluntarily chosen commitments. For one of the finest features of love is its initiative. Our response as a Christian to God's initiative in Jesus Christ will take flesh in the initiatives which we have taken with his grace in order to make charity shine out in the midst of men.

APPENDIX I: THE PROCEDURE FOR ENCOUNTER

The basis for all encounter is a desire for relationship, and a knowledge or "inkling" of the value of communion. The person "on the road" or "going to encounter" must realize that he is presenting his freedom to enter itself into communion with an-

179

other freedom. The fundamental procedure is that of dialogue. There are three steps.

The person must first listen to the call given by the partner; this will be given in a sign, as an expression of his freedom. He must then analyze the experience which this call arouses in him; this experience is expressive mainly of continuity and shock.

Secondly, he must examine the orientations which this contact may take. He must make a provisional response to the partner, and express his point of view. He must try to become enlightened about the aim and conditions which would result from each orientation considered.

Thirdly, he must live in communion with his partner.

A general criterion to be observed—we have been talking especially about encounter with God—is that God's point of view must be shared, and that it must be seen as crystallized in the life of Jesus Christ.

In the catechesis of encounter, the catechist must play the role of a discreet intermediary in the dialogue between his students and God. For their part, the students must learn to open themselves, to judge themselves, and to trust themselves and others.

By way of simplification, we have spoken of three dimensions in encounter, namely, objectivity, subjectivity, and intersubjectivity. A closer look, however, shows that the third category is actually a specification of the second. For this reason, the procedure for encounter is also a specification of values. In particular, there is a relation between the desire for encounter and the value of communion.

Moreover, the connection between values and situations being given, the procedure for encounter is also a specification of the procedure for the interpretation of a situation.

"Situation" here means that a freedom offers to enter itself into communion with another freedom.

The stages of procedure aiming directly at encounter are the three movements (or rhythmic moments) of the dialogue. Therefore, both partners must be considered at each stage, and so must the effects of their progressive contact.

1. So that the *call* to the first partner, who in catechesis is God, may be distinguished, the catechist must bring out the signs constituting mediations in which God presented himself. It is not enough to put the catechized in touch with the materiality of the sign; it is necessary that this sign be shown as the call from a person. It is on this level that interpersonal experience is situated.

Now, this first contact usually arouses a "mixed" experience. On the one hand, the gift which God wishes to give appears in the line of continuity of what man naturally desires, and the Lord prepares his superior gifts by inferior ones which are parables of them. On the other hand, God is always surprising to man, for he asks him to purify and broaden his own expectancy. For this reason, the first stage of encounter with God is also a shock for man. Besides, it is this "distance" which brings about the second movement of the dialogue.

The catechist, therefore, will help the catechized to remove the obstacles to their encounter with God. Some examples of obstacles are distraction and self-centeredness. The catechist will encourage his students to make positive preparation: attention and openness to God. But above all he will show his students that it is normal that the first encounter with the Word of God calls forth questions.

2. The questions which the catechized put forth will in fact be provisional answers to God's call. They will tell God what they are experiencing, what causes them joy and what is filling them with fear; they will ask for more light on the orientations wherein the encounter may be developed.

The whole Gospel is at the disposal of the catechized for the use of finding enlightenment. Jesus is offering here more explicitly the divine gift of a superior life, a richer and definitively happy life. He also very frankly specifies the conditions and the requirements for attaining it. Since man's present situation is not exempt from the temptations in which his own unruly passions hold him, the way of the Gospel is strewn with difficulties. This means that, during the second movement of the dialogue, man is confronted with the possibility of making a "surpassing"; this requires, and in fact is, conversion. Both the history of the Gospel and the Church show us what are the consequences of the different attitudes adopted by men in answering God's call.

3. In the dialogue between persons, who are imperfect and who therefore have something to learn from each other, the first two movements usually consist in the successive exchanges of the two points of view, the third movement being a mutual enrichment and at the same time a correction of the two initial respective positions.

Man's dialogue with God presents analogies with the human dialogue, but it has characteristics which make it radically different. God's radical ontological priority, which is already at work in some way in the first two movements of the dialogue, is decisive for the third.

Man's option between the orientations he has distinguished in the second movement is good when, at least in principle, his way of seeing is radically oriented towards consonance with God's way of seeing. God, of course, being magnificently patient, the immediate need is often only a step, still very imperfect, in the right direction—namely, communion.

Communion realized through a truly lived encounter consists in man's active participation in the "authentic" knowledge which God is communicating to him. This communion is transforming for man, and it is developed in a continual process of welcomed call and committing response, in a vital rhythm of comprehension and mutual gift of self.

The concrete criterion for this option consists in the life itself of Jesus Christ, which is at once God's definite call and man's perfect response.

APPENDIX II: FREEDOM

Of all our desires, the most intent psychologically is the desire to be free from all constraint coming from another, and especially from impersonal law. This is a negative aspect of liberty. The first step in a catechesis of freedom, therefore, is to recognize that this negative aspect (free *from*) only has value in reference to a positive aspect: free *for*.

There are different levels at which this positive freedom, this desire which seeks to realize itself, this interior dynamism, can be situated. It can, on the one hand, be situated at a physical and psychic level, and in both a negative and a positive sense: negatively, in the desire to be free from every exterior bond which holds back or drags along; positively, in the desire to deploy to the full one's physical and psychic vitality.

On the other hand, it can be situated on a spiritual level, in the desire to realize a good recognized as such by the intelligence; in the desire to master one's instinctive and psychic wants so as to keep them dependent on a desire which has worth in the rational order; above all, in the desire to achieve a capacity to become engaged in an interpersonal relationship, a dynamism of conscious self-realization, especially a love in which each partner recognizes the personal worth of the other.

Rational knowledge and the spiritual will demand that the physical and psychic desires be kept in place. Even so, we feel within ourselves an opposition to this worth-while natural order: at such and such a moment we are tempted to follow in an unbridled (that is to say, absolute) way this or that physical or psychic desire. Moreover, it happens that we yield to this instinctive urge which drives us outside the human order as it is expressed in the moral law (whether natural or positive).

Freedom is validly exercised when it is turned towards the good. My freedom, which is the interior dynamism which enables me to realize myself spiritually, is genuine when it leaves all egocentricity behind it, and is tuned in to life in relationship with others. This spiritual freedom is possessed by every man, either in a state of growth or of decrease; its evolution depends on psychological age, sociological circumstance, and especially on the actual exercise of whatever degree of freedom we already have.

A consequence of the exercise of this freedom is that a viable connection is established between spiritual (interior freedom) and autonomy (liberty with regard to personal law). The growth of the capacity to make a personal moral judgment and to act according to this judgment, normally should go hand in hand with autonomy with regard to laws experienced as imposed from without. But by the same token, the lawfulness of autonomy is conditioned by the capacity to judge rationally and to carry out by oneself these rational judgments. All freedom is genuine freedom only when it is directed to good. Freely to do evil is to make a caricature of one's own freedom.

Other questions also arise in connection with freedom, for example social freedom (in particular, the liberation from social structures in which some men normally have no access to economic means and so find themselves deprived of that actual exercise of liberty which consists in a choice of values). Or again, there are many questions which arise concerning political liberty. However, our work here is to examine still more closely the question of spiritual freedom.

A synthesis between the two levels on which the freedom of the Christian is exercised is achieved in three steps. We can list them under the headings "The Plan of God," "Difficulties," and "Christian Realization."

The Plan of God. The plan of God, very simply, is that there be an harmonious unity between the two levels of freedom, or rather, in the exercise of freedom on the two levels. The gift of supernatural life implies a capacity for supernatural freedom, so that man can enter freely into communion with God. This supernatural strength helps us to coordinate all our human actions towards this union with God.

Difficulties. These difficulties are due to breaks in continuity. Religion, and especially supernatural religion, demands that we should recognize the part that God plays in the life of a free man.

We must be aware, therefore, of a tendency in ourselves not to admit that God plays a part in our life. This is due either to a desire for "absolute" liberty (pride), to want to be perfect without God, to not want to admit that our free acts do not originate of themselves, but that they are created by God and must be directed according to the order willed by God for the good of man. Or else it is because we are not firm in the reliance of our freedom on God (weakness). When grace does not help us in time to overcome completely our temptations, we are inclined to relax our free efforts to collaborate with God. In light of this, therefore, we must learn to practice a detachment with regard to these tendencies towards pride, impatience, or an easy yielding of our inclinations.

We must also be aware that we sometimes refuse this detachment and so introduce sin into our lives, as a willful misdirection of our freedom. If we refuse this detachment, moreover, we are freely abandoning ourselves to the slavery of sin.

Finally, we must always refer ourselves in our difficulties to Christ. Jesus exercised his freedom in order to be faithful to his Father. He met the obstacles which men placed in the way of his mission. But he accepted this struggle willingly, in a love faithful to the death on the cross. We must follow Christ, and for this following we must first be converted. In the context of liberty, this means that we must recognize the true significance of our freedom, the direction it requires, its limits, and its positive possibilities when we rely on grace. From the moment of this conversion of mentality, we accept an interior struggle against the deviations of our liberty, and a struggle in the world whenever there is opposition to the Christian mentality.

Christian Realization. This is actually a "going beyond." Jesus risen from the dead communicates to us his strength. He sends us his Holy Spirit, who leads us to recognize better our spiritual freedom and who makes it grow when we exercise it faithfully. "For the law of the Spirit of life in Christ Jesus has set me free from the law of sin and death" (Rom. 8, 2). We live in growth towards the fullness of freedom which will be given to us in heaven, for it has been promised to the sons of God. We receive a foretaste of this perfect realization in several ways—when, for example, we experience a free attachment, enlightened and faithful, to the values of the kingdom of God; or when, among all the deficiencies of our liberty, we yet remain trusting in God and in the mediation of Christ.

This "paschal" freedom, for this is the level of Christian freedom, —this liberty in growth, is a particpation in the very freedom of God, who realizes the perfection of freedom-directed-to-communion.

APPENDIX III: "HONEST TO GOD"

The great stir caused by Anglican Bishop John A. T. Robinson's book *Honest to God* is sufficient reason for us to consider it here. The basic problem Robinson raises is how we can best encounter God, either first of all by specifying, after natural reflection and in the light of the truths of revelation, the contents and represensations of our thoughts about God, and then examining our way of encountering him; or else having a certain experience of God encounter, and then reviewing our mental representations about this encounter, and finally to try to perfect that encounter.

For Robinson, God is not identical with the world, but on the other hand God exists only in the world. If this is so, however, then we must acquire a different conception of divine transcendence than that which puts God "up there" or "out there." Those persons who have made this change in conception, at least by abandoning their old one, seek God in "religion," which itself must be conceived of in a different way: as not consisting in taking care of the profane world. Men of our time, however, are incapable of abandoning their interest in the world and in their neighbor.

Therefore, another, more efficacious conception of God is established. "To open ourself to another *unconditionally* in love *is* to be with him in the presence of God . . . it may not be consciously Christian, but it may be a meeting of Christ in that man, because his humanity is acception *without any reservation*" (pp. 99–100).* Modern man also seeks in Christianity a "total commitment of charity" in the world. Because God is in the world, God is the ground of our being. Christ came to teach us, by his example, that the supreme and unique law of life is the "unconditional" commitment of charity. God is wholly in Christ, for God is charity, and Christ manifests unconditional charity. From these conceptions about God, we must also alter our conceptions of prayer and morality.

In addition to new ways of conceiving of God and Christ, there is also a new way of conceiving of the encounter with God in the world. The "sacred" character of the liturgy should be conceived of as the presence of God in what is profane. This is reality lived without consciousness of its own depth; the "sacred" is itself the depth of the profane, a depth lived consciously. Thus the Eucharist is charity lived "*in sacris*" and expressing itself symbolically, that is, expressed in a meal of bread and wine, lived according to the total depth of Christian charity.

Non-liturgical prayer also undergoes an analogous transformation. It is no longer a question of withdrawing from the world to

* Since the paperback edition of *Honest to God* is the one most in use, our page references are to that edition, published in Philadelphia by The Westminster Press, 1963. The italics are our own.

pray, but of realizing the duty of charity towards our neighbor as our true vocation, a vocation of "unconditional commitment" where we meet God. There may indeed still be calmer and more concentrated moments, but they only serve to make us more conscious of the encounter already made in fraternal charity, which must ever be perfected.

There is a certain parallel between the insights of Bishop Robinson and our thoughts in our chapter on charity. We, while keeping in mind from the very beginning that man is capable of encountering God only in mediations, have taken as the basis of our reflection at once the personal transcendence of God (since it is he who must be personally encountered) and his immanence in the world (since mediations are part of the world). The world is never separated from God, but its relations to God may be either explicit for man (encounter with God in the sacred) or implicit (encounter in the profane). Praying encounter in the profane requires encounter in the sacred, since our attention to the presence of God is basic to prayer.

Robinson has the very "honest" intention of encouraging, among our contemporaries who live in an active relationship with the world, the encounter with God who is not identical with the world. However, because of several of his expressions and tendencies, the author is obscure about much of the twofold problem posed by God's immanent transcendence.

Does Bishop Robinson, for example, still conceive of God transcending in the way of a personal Being? Or is it our existence which possesses a divine dimension, a dynamism tending towards a perfect charity which goes beyond man? He says that the affirmation as well as the negation of a Being who would be a Person outside of our personal existence, is foreign to the manner of thinking which he advocates. He would oppose every concept of person which would introduce into the infinity of God any limitations of an individuality such as it suits our limited being, or which would exclude God's immanence in the world.

In our opinion, however, it is important to state clearly that God is not identical with our deepest being. Our existential depth consists in our relationship with God. Because of his personal infinity, God is also personally Another, and even the Total Other, for man.

The same ambiguity of expression—which permits, therefore, of diverging interpretations—is found in Robinson's discussion of Jesus Christ. God is wholly in Jesus, yes, but it what sense? Is Jesus merely the perfect human realization of unconditional charity, and thereby the perfect realization of the divine, or is he personally God? Does his resurrection mean only that this perfect realization continues to have an influence in the Church (especially during the celebration of the Eucharist), notably in its influence on the practice of charity, or does Jesus the risen Lord live as a Person?

This ambiguity of terms is again found in Robinson's thoughts on man's encounter with God in his neighbor. The basis of this contact with the divine resides in the unconditional commitment of charity. However, is the motive justifying this unconditional commitment, the absoluteness of it all, —is it proper more to the neighbor, or more to fraternal charity, at least as an absolute aim? Or is this motive precisely the relativeness of the neighbor, which means that fraternal charity is not an absolute in itself? Or is it a relativeness which helps us to discover the Other, to whom man is related, and which would make of man a "mediation" of God for man?

In other words, and we will make them serve as our conclusion, by means of a "reducing" tendency (which especially reduces the whole of reality to relationships between man and the world, and above all to inter-human relationships), man must first of all reach an unconditional commitment towards his neighbor. This realization would procure for him the experience of the divine, that is to say, the encounter with God in the neighbor. Pushed to the extreme, this tendency leads either to a Promethean conception of morality, or to a pantheistic conception of existence. Robinson certainly does not go quite so far. For him, man only becomes capable of this unconditional commitment through conversion, and through grace received. But we ought to know God, the author of this grace, before encountering him in brotherly love. God must already have been encountered in a manifestation, a revelation, which comes from God himself. It is this which underlines the other tendency.

According to the "open" tendency, notably the going-beyond relationships between man and the world, as well as those between man himself, man receives, already in a certain way in his natural experience, but in a particular way in Jesus Christ, the message of charity which goes beyond human strength.

It is true that a man who consciously follows the way of human charity can be unconsciously "on the road to God." The needs of charity, felt with increasing perfection, will perhaps even help him to know God beforehand as an "anonymous," or to know him in an "anonymous" way. Yet man rids himself of the ambiguity between human sufficiency and the discovery of the true God only by passing beyond the world.

It is in passing beyond the consideration of what men and the world are in themselves (this requires conversion), it is in going forward in the direction towards which the relativeness of creatures points, it is in discovering in sacred mediations (making their relation to Another explicit), and especially in Jesus Christ, the action of God, —it is in all this that, first of all, man encounters God, in the full meaning of that word. Then, from this "gift" received in an encounter which, psychologically, for a dialectical moment, "God alone" counts, man becomes capable of encountering God again in the profane encounter.

Then, of course, but more and more fully, the relationships between men can become mediations of divine and human charity, communicated to us by Jesus Christ.

X

Eschatology

1. GOD'S WORD

The Bible

The entire Bible concerns the union of men with God. It reveals in a progressive way how this union was established and in what it consists in—in growth towards perfection in Christ, through the Holy Spirit, who communicates divine charity.

From the Old Testament we learn of the original vocation: God with man in the Garden of Eden. But sin breaks this union. The path of redemption, however, eventually leads to the "blessing," which is the promise of restoration in the kingdom of God. We first see this promise of a kingdom in a terrestrial perspective, but as the notion becomes purified, we see that it is the eternal kingdom only which is the essential one.

As for the New Testament, we must keep in mind that the Gospel was written in the light of Christ's resurrection. The whole story of the Messiah is centered around his Pasch. His return at the end of time is announced at the completion of the Pasch for his followers. The Acts of the Apostles, the epistles, and the Book of Revelation insist on the relation of the Parousia to the universal resurrection.

All the New Testament writings show that the "coming" of Christ—notably in his public life, in his death and resurrection, in his action of sending the Spirit, and in his promise to return at the end of time—constitutes "one coherent event." This is why this "coming" is "actual" throughout the history of the Church and for every Christian. Moreover, the basic identity of the mystery of the Pasch (Pasch-and-Parousia) is affirmed in the lack of clearness about when this second coming will happen, and in the fact that the Pasch is to be celebrated "for the duration."

The Scriptures present the final and complete reunion between God and man less as the result of man's growth in virtue than as the result of the definitive intervention of God. God accomplishes his plan, he reveals his glory. He repairs what had been lost, and he makes everything "new," everything "different." He does this in Christ and through men. We must hope in this definitive intervention of God. We pray that "thy kingdom come," so that then we can "be with him forever" (1 Tim. 4, 17). We must be ready to receive this final gift, which will be given to those who "live in Christ."

The Liturgy

All liturgical prayer is directed towards the glory of God in all its radiance. Moreover, the central event both in the sacraments and in the liturgical year is the commemoration of Christ's Pasch. The eucharistic celebration is done in union with the risen Christ. It is an anticipation of the celestial union.

In the liturgy for the sick and for the dead, we find a mixture of elements, some closer to the "eschatological" mentality of the early Christians, others stressing "preparation" (or the lack of it) pertaining to the terrestrial structure of the kingdom.

Life Witness

In our catechesis, we should make use of the reactions of certain Christians to great earthly success and failure, and also the attitudes of saints and holy men and women in the face of death. As for the religious state, we can point out those communities whose way of life brings out most forcibly the eschatological dimension of Christ's religion, or the lives of those saints whose eschatological limits are the more dramatic—the life of Brother Charles de Foucauld, for instance. In all cases, we should stress the paschal character—the life-death-resurrection—of Christian life.

Reflection and Formulation

Problems that arise in this connection can be placed under three headings: the final situation itself; the transition from here to there, which is death; and the relations of continuity and discontinuity between the terrestrial and eschatological values.

1. The essential content of eschatology consists in the final situation. We are capable of thinking of what surpasses our present (but not final) situation, because our spirit surpasses our earthly condition; but we have great difficulty in conceiving of this future state, because our thought has immediately to rely on aspects of our present situation.

Our future will be accomplished on two levels: that of human existence as such, whose "end" will surpass the limits of growth; and that of the level of God's supernatural gift, for the final gift will surpass all earlier supernatural gifts. In catechesis, we must stress this second surpassing. We should not try to discover in advance the secret of God, whose liberal bounty wishes to give us this last surprise. Let us prepare (in our present preparation) to receive this full gift. As for the first surpassing, it bears upon the "plenitude" which will repair the imperfections of our actual existence of "becoming." It is to think of the positive "end" of our human condition.

Our existence of becoming on earth is marked by conditions of time and space. Hence there is double difficulty in how to think of temporal duration transformed into eternal duration, and of space as we know it now into a new field of existence and action. We must first point out the ambiguity of these two conditions of earthly existence, and then extend their perfection to plenitude.

Terrestrial space is a factor of perfection and of imperfection; it is in the "mediation" of localized bodies that human minds are conscious of themselves, and are in conscious relations with each other; but it is the distance from bodies, or their "rivalry" to occupy the same space, which prevents perfect consciousness and relations. We do not know clearly what corresponds for bodies transformed by the resurrection, to the localization of bodies not yet transformed. Perhaps we may speak analogically of a "new" space, which will permit everyone to be "together," without proximity being crowded, or distance deprivative from the contact point of view. It is undoubtedly better to avoid expressions of "space" in catechesis (Where is heaven? Where is Mary at this moment?), and to surpass them by speaking rather of a "field of action.") This brings us nearer to the categories now used in the sciences of matter. These are discovering more and more the amplitude and coherence of the cosmic forces and their radiation in different fields of action. With less imagination (the modern sciences are less imaginative), and more penetration into the real, we can perceive the function of risen bodies, as the perfection of what we knew imperfectly here below: the mediation of fully human consciousness and interpersonal relations.

As to terrestrial time, it also contains perfection and imperfection. "Now" I know the past (more or less forgotten) and the future (foreseen more or less clearly); but I have not got the fully concentrated knowledge of my whole existence. Eternity will give me that, without excluding the variety of life at the very interior of this plenitude.

The way in which we can think of the last realities and grasp sound formulations of them, starts from our actual experience of our earthly situation, in which the divine plan of salvation is being gradually worked out.

Neither for protology nor eschatology have we a "report" made by witnesses fully "attuned" to the condition of the life in question. For when the disciples saw the risen Christ (as we have testimony in the New Testament), they themselves did not enter the conditions of the risen life. Their senses miraculously perceived the manifestation Christ made of himself. As to the new properties manifested, they precisely concern the powers of the risen Lord to effect a more perfect communication of himself when and where he chose; and the disappearance of this communication stresses the fact that we are not yet fully attuned to this other condition of life.

Reflection, then, proceeds from actual experience, by projections towards the first start, and last end; each projection requires some correction, since it is not a question of quantitative likeness but of qualitative analogies.

Knowledge of protology develops according to the knowledge of the whole Christian mystery, for the "initial" situation is understood as the basic starting point of the redeemer's saving action. Equally, knowledge of eschatology (final situation) develops according to penetration into the paschal mystery. This is true of adult faith compared with childish faith; and, with differences, of the development of the formulation of dogma in the history of the Church.

2. Death as the transition from life on earth to the afterlife raises several very important questions. It is the duty of catechesis,

195

therefore, to distinguish those which are of great importance from those of less importance. Catechesis, for instance, has no real concern about the different opinions over the biological aspects of death. At most, it could point out that on this level of transition, from cellular life to cellular decay, death is not reduced to some instantaneous moment that is the same in all cases. Catechesis will instead draw attention to the fact that there is in death a transition between two states, one belonging to our earthly condition, the other to our state beyond it. After this transition takes place, there will be no changing of attitudes.

However, if this transition is not endured unconsciously, but comes to be a reality which man in his freedom can approach in a choice of ways, then two further considerations must be taken into account. The first is that death is not only a fact or event which man endures *regardless* of his liberty. Conscious death is an act to be accepted in advance and realized with liberty, and we mean that liberty whose consent or dissent has a decisive role to play in the direction of the transition from life on earth to the afterlife.

Seen thus, death is the act which can *concentrate* in itself all our interior life, with approval or disapproval, and also concentrate our whole orientation as regards the final solution into which God introduces us.

Christ is the prototype of the Christian, and also of the dying Christian, who shares in the redeeming mystery of Christ's death. The dying Christ is the prototype of the dying Christian.

It must not be denied that from a certain point of view, death is the final failure of all earthly realization, but it must be stated just as categorically that every failure on earth is not any ultimate failure on man's part. On the contrary, all suffering, which has a close relationship to death, can be accepted in a Christian way, and become the way to full realization of one's Christian life.

3. The relations which exist between life on earth and life hereafter are those of continuity in discontinuity. This is why we

prefer to present them here in a schematic form, while at the same time making evident their dialectic structure.

Our thesis, then, is that there is in death already the same basic reality: grace, which is participation in the life of the glorified Christ, through the communication of his Spirit.

But the antithesis reads: There is not yet in death that complete and definitive gift—which is much more than a mere increase. It is transcendent, it will come as a new and different gift, surpassing the powers of our imagination. It will be given only on condition that we undergo a break in life, which is to say, that we can receive this gift only through death with Christ, in accepting the failure of every earthly form of our existence (this is the death of the cosmos), in living in sufficient detachment and struggling against sin.

Our synthesis, therefore, must see death as the journeying towards accomplishment in glorious liberty (Rom. 8, 21).

According to the general law of development of this "journeying towards," there must first of all be a life situation which will mature so that the new gift may be eventually welcomed in as comprehensive a way as possible. This gift allows for anticipation of it, though it also makes allowances for setbacks. We might compare this maturation process with the rhythm of natural or animal development: life, death, new birth. Our life in grace follows an analogous rhythm: God comes to crown his first gifts, which man has been using, in order to transform man's life.

This continual transformation is brought about in two ways, or rather, it is seen from two points of view, depending on whether the Christian lives his life in the Church in the lay or in the religious state.

In the former state, grace gives the Christian the strength of superanimation in order to realize earthly values more perfectly. It also helps to mature his disposition to welcome the full and ultimate gift. It is the incarnation of charity in its terrestrial perspective. This is Christian life considered as the preparation of welcome in view of transformation.

In the latter state, grace is provided in order to give the Christian the strength to realize some of his anticipations. The Eucharist is the first of these anticipations—the meeting with the glorified Christ in the ecclesial community of charity. Following from this, grace is seen as the incarnation of charity as the prefiguration of heavenly modes, notably in sacramental life; in the states of life structured on the evangelical counsels; and in eschatological acts and in an evolution of attitude which is realized more perfectly in the lay Christian state. This is Christian life considered as the prefiguration, partially anticipated, of the ultimate gift.

2. THE HUMAN BACKGROUND

We have already taken modern ways of thinking into consideration in our theological reflections. Now, besides these, we shall point out a few of the stronger and some of the weaker factors in the modern-day attitude towards life and death.

Psychology

Among the factors favorable to a Christian eschatological attitude are the need of modern man to find a satisfying solution to the great problems of life—a solution which will provide a general vision of life considered as a whole, making of life a coherent unity; his sense of history, which he sees as developing towards a definite end; and his desire to see the formation of a perfect community made up of all nations and peoples.

The difficulties for modern man arise chiefly from the transcendent character of eschatology. Therefore, catechesis ought especially to bring out the "reality" of this "other" world, which has "already begun." Revelation is not meant to satisfy our curiosity about the modes of accomplishment, however. Through biblical images, then, we must strive to penetrate to the personal kernel: to be with the Lord always. Psychoanalysis, of course, can present many objections to the Christian belief in the "other" world. Our catechesis must counter these objections by presenting the true data of our eschatological faith, especially the resurrection of the Lord.

There is also the double temptation for modern man of allowing himself to be drawn away by earthly enjoyment, and wishing to procure happiness through human endeavor alone. In our catechesis, therefore, we must encourage in our students an attitude of welcome towards the final gift which will come from God.

Sociology

A more subtle difficulty is presented in the well-meant anxiety of modern man about temporal, social matters. Here as elsewhere, of course, there are no simple solutions, but as a general counter principle for our catechesis we ought to show that the crown of all social activity is the full realization of charity. This is not merely to say that "love conquers all"—for too often the attitude here is that love is oblivious to or even inconsiderate of many human problems—but that the love of Christ can transform all things.

Several other questions in this connection relate to the incomplete development of a man's liberty. We should distinguish, therefore, between the liberty accompanying the awakening of reason, and that needed for a definite taking up of a position.* All our progress in the life of grace leads to obtaining "the glorious liberty of the children of God" (Rom. 8, 21). We should not forget, finally, that the development of a Christian eschatologi-

* *Summa Theol.,* II II, q. 189, a. 5.

cal outlook can only be achieved also through the experience of joy and sorrow transformed into the joy and sorrow of Christ.

3. COMMUNICATING THE MESSAGE

Preparation

The whole of our catechesis must be so structured that the general line is truly oriented towards eschatology. This is to say that the course must be based on the development of the mystery of salvation. Moreover, since eschatology is the basic theme, each part of the course must also be presented in an eschatological perspective.

Concerning the eschatological subjects themselves, we recommend the following "stresses." First, we take as our starting point the fact of Christ's resurrection. Then the death of the Christian is put in explicit relation to the death of Christ and the meaning of his death. Next, we point out that the last judgment has already begun, since it concerns our position towards Christ; this position is incarnated especially in our charity or in the want of it towards our neighbor. Then we show that purgatory is a purification of charity, painful and consoling at the same time. The next step is to show that revelation on hell is not meant to torture us. On the contrary, it helps us to understand the seriousness of the position which we choose to take up towards the charity which comes from God. Only those go to hell who "die in the state of mortal sin"—that is, who do not accept to retract a willful consent to commit mortal sin and who harden in this right up until the very time of transition to eternity.

After this, we should speak of heaven in personal terms, of the beatifying "meeting," of blessed "communion." Finally, we must be both reserved and explicit about the resurrection of the body. We must be reserved in that we should avoid unqualified statements or descriptions as if they had no analogous character. We must be explicit in that we must not give the impression that only "souls" count for God. We must love his whole creation, and be aware that we, whom he created, are helped by him to grow towards completion and final communion with him, in Jesus Christ.

Procedure

We must take care always to use biblical expressions in their original context. This especially concerns those images which show the journey of God's people towards perfect union with him.

Moreover, we must present Christ's resurrection in a concrete manner, that is, we must place the accomplishment in the perspective of the whole divine plan of salvation, as "something surpassing." In other words, Christ's resurrection must never be presented in an anthropological perspective (as if everything that mattered was a happiness which man would reach by his own means), but rather in a "doxological perspective," where everything is seen to be oriented towards God's glory, everything expresses his goodness towards us. We must also view the resurrection in a Christocentric perspective," that the accomplishment is the participation of all in the complete realization of Christ.

We must throw light on what will be "negative" in the afterlife, showing that everything pertaining to imperfection, especially sin, will disappear. In heaven there will be no more suffering and death, no uncertainty, no lack of clearness, no interior anguish, no disagreement among men, no resistance to grace, no powerlessness to respond fully to God's love, as Christ has revealed it to us. Hell, on the contrary, is the imprisonment forever in all these evils.

In a positive way we must explain, dynamically, how personal and community values will be lived to perfection; how man, soul and body, will be entirely saved and blessed; how his stabilized liberty will be absolutely engaged towards good; how all creation will be renewed and set in order forever; how all will meet together in joy, and in an unending communion where the glory of God will radiate in all its splendor; how, in the charity which the Spirit will communicate to us, we will live forever with God in Christ.

It does not suffice, in our catechesis, to enlighten the student's reflections by presenting notional modes of thought and categories of systematic philosophy as they concern man's end. It is much more important to help the students' reflection develop according to sapiential modes. As the Divine Master clearly taught us to do in the Gospel, we will praise the value judgment of that man who esteems eternal life above any purely terrestrial realization. We will proclaim as blessed that man who receives access to the plenitude of the gift of God.

In these perspectives, it is possible for us continually to appeal to the students' activity: where can they find expression of the eschatological realities in the Scripture, in the liturgy, in the testimony of Christians? What comparisons can they make between their expression of happiness and their sense of heaven (and, respectively, between unhappiness and hell)? What does the need of being completely delivered from sin, and being perfectly united to God, mean for them? Do they celebrate Easter as the beginning of their resurrection with Christ?

How will they take into account the accomplishment of salvation, so as to answer the complaint of people in need, and the contemporary inquiry into the meaning of life?

How will they proclaim in their prayer their orientation towards the accomplishment of the Christian mystery?

They will proclaim it in this way: "I believe in the everlasting life." The everlasting life is the life of perfect charity in communion with God, in our Lord, Jesus Christ.

Conclusion

THROUGHOUT the two volumes which end here, our aim has been to assemble the data which seemed to us to be the most important in promoting an encounter with the Lord.

This task required organic unity. Hence we have indicated first the "structures" of this unity, and then the succinct presentation of "themes" according to their essential aspects, for the structures would be meaningless if they were not utilized in the exposition of themes which in turn find a reciprocal possibility of development in the former.

The reader will be well aware of the toil entailed by this type of research. May this fact encourage him in pursuing the effort of thought which is required of him. The author, who recalls how certain discoveries were made, interprets these with gratitude as blessings of divine providence, as "graces" received sometimes unpredictably and in the most difficult circumstances.

Our aim is to help bring about an encounter with the Lord. It is he who constantly takes the initiative in this encounter. He disposes us to desire it, and in so doing takes the first step by addressing us. This reality, which is always actual, must be understood in a much richer sense than if we were merely referring to certain spoken words. It is true, of course, that God caused his Son made man to pronounce certain human words which are in fact divine. But this restricted sense of the term must be interpreted in a much wider context of meaning. That is why we have so often underlined the intrinsic relationships which must be recognized between the priority of lived reality, which has its own significance and needs to be experienced, whether directly or indirectly; and the role of elucidation, or formulation, so as to allow for the human completeness of this experience and the control of its inner interpretation.

Accordingly, it is the very life of Jesus Christ, or his person expressed by his acts, which preeminently remains the Word of God. Although we can distinguish the meaning of this life more clearly through his spoken words, these must always be interpreted in their living context.

This same Jesus, Word of God, equally provides a perfect answer for man. It is an existential answer, made in the name of all mankind, and all men are invited to seek to integrate their answer within it. Therefore, all must listen to God in Jesus Christ and respond to God in Jesus Christ. Then will the Lord complete his undertaking and bring us into communion with him.

In order that this life may be realized in dialogue, the Spirit has been communicated to the Church. In this Church God has established two privileged and complementary paths to encounter with him: the Bible and the liturgy. Liturgy equally represents speech to the extent that its symbolic gestures are utterances. Jesus Christ is the central point of the Bible as he is of the liturgy. He is also at the center of the third way to encounter, though it is less privileged from certain points of view but more decisive from others, namely, the way of living testimony followed throughout the history of the Church and even to this day. For the Head operates and makes himself known in his faithful members.

These testimonies of Christian life prolong the existential path of the Bible. Does God also address us through events which relate to our worldly existence? We have already considered in which sense these events differ in kind from human actions directly inspired by the love of God in providing a manifestation of this love, and in which sense each situation, in particular each new situation, represents a summons from God to the Church in each one of us.

Therefore, God addresses us; he speaks personally by means of different signs which must be mainly understood in their total context. But many are those who scarcely recognize God's signs for what they are, and all of us are tempted on occasion to interpret them in terms of our immediate gain, instead of seeking that interpretation which must conform our views to those of the Lord. This explains why God makes use of interpreters. The whole of catechetics is precisely at the service of God's Word. We use the term "catechetics" in the generic sense, since, once the necessary preparations have been made, it entails the twofold and essential task of proclaiming and interpreting God's word, that is to say, of completely illuminating the signs of God and of making their authentic significance explicit. Faithfulness to this task requires respect for the forms of expression chosen by God and a careful handling of the context in which they find their true meaning. This is particularly true of the general context which deals with the development of the mystery of salvation and in which we incorporate our daily life.

In this case, too, God has provided certain guarantees within his Church. All religious instruction is imparted in accordance with the magisterium. Nevertheless, the task of interpretation belongs to the entire ecclesiastical community and can never be considered as static and inert formulation, for the entire Church must grow in the knowledge of God's word. This progress requires us to revise our mentality periodically together with the expressions which serve to formulate Christ's message in different situations. One of the important elements of each new situation is the type of category according to which men think, in relation to their turn of mind and their experience.

A similar awareness of actuality and of the paths followed by the word of God directs our heart and our mind towards the content of this word. The Lord informs us which relationships he wishes to develop, in the living context between him and ourselves, so that we may discover happiness. He reminds us that our situation is made up of disorderly elements, and he tells us that Jesus Christ saves us. He therefore summons us to welcome redemption and to participate in it, so that it may apply to our entire personal life and to the whole of mankind. For within redemption itself, the relationships desired by God are manifested in every direction, in their depth, their breadth, and their height, thus receiving their true name: charity.

This living content of God's active word, his love—manifested in Jesus Christ, incarnated, crucified, and risen—communicated by the Spirit so that all men may participate in God's life, this existential content which is essentially realized through the existential way of Christ, provides the core of all the chapters of this work. We are of the opinion that a mode of thought particularly suited to this content of the Christian message resides in a dialectical method: extension, discontinuity, transcendence.

Catechetics must always aim at the participation of the whole man in the incarnation, in the cross, and in the resurrection of Jesus Christ. For these three represent the path of salvation: attraction, conversion, communion. Attraction is provided by extending the development of human values, although the fact may not always be obvious; conversion is necessary in order to correct deviations tending towards anthropocentricity; communion with God on a superior plane integrates human values "in a different way." This path is the only one which allows the dynamism of the charity which radiates from Christ to take life within us and develop.

206

When we consider this fact, these forms, and this content of God's word, we must acknowledge that the dialogue which God invites us to hold with him is also primarily of an existential nature. No doubt, we will have to use "words" on occasion in our conversation with God: our faith, which has become a meditation of the signs of God in his presence, will be expressed in formulated prayer, so that we may tell God that we have heard his summons and ask him for the necessary strength to respond fully. But dialogue is primarily made up of this attentiveness and this response in the context of life itself. "To live in dialogue with God" means to transform life itself into a fulfillment of the love which is an interpersonal relationship developing by means of a constant dialogic movement of welcoming and responding. This dialogue is lived because interpersonal exchange is founded on the knowledge of a gift received and reciprocated as an expression of the persons involved. Thus we recall what Jesus has said of "life": it consists in "knowing" God and him whom God has sent, for to know a person entirely means to experience the love which unites us to him.

The dialogue held between man and God and the dialogue which men hold together must be reunited. The Spirit breathes where it will and as it wills. It is not for us to draw up a blueprint showing how this reunion can take place.

Our Christian vocation, in which we find our joy, must always consist in listening to God who addresses us, no matter how his word reaches us; in deepening the meaning of this word by faith through prayer, that is, by responding throughout our life; and by disseminating this word in the service of Christ, each according to his role or in collaboration with others, so that all may participate in the communion into which this dialogue brings us.